Promises from God for Women of Color
Copyright 2001

Published by:
Nia Publishing
2440 Fairburn Road, Suite 103
Atlanta, GA 30331

Scripture quotations are taken from the *Holy Bible,* King
James Version

Some material has been taken from the *Women of Color Study
Bible*, copyright 1999 by Nia Publishing.

NIA PUBLISHING is an African-American owned company
based in Atlanta, GA. Started in 1993 by Mel Banks, Jr., former
marketing director for Urban Ministries, Inc., its first product
was *The Children of Color Bible, King James Version* which
has sold over 250,000 copies to date. The ownership, employ-
ees, and products of Nia Publishing are dedicated to the cul-
tural and spiritual growth of people of color, as individuals in
the community and in the church.

Produced by The Livingstone Corporation
Project Staff include: Katie E. Gieser and Christopher D. Hudson
Typeset by Joyce Schram

Printed and bound in the United States of America

Table of Contents

FAMILY ISSUES

ATTRIBUTES OF GOD

RELATIONSHIP ISSUES

WHAT THE BIBLE SAYS ABOUT. . .

TRIALS AND TROUBLES

The Christian Life

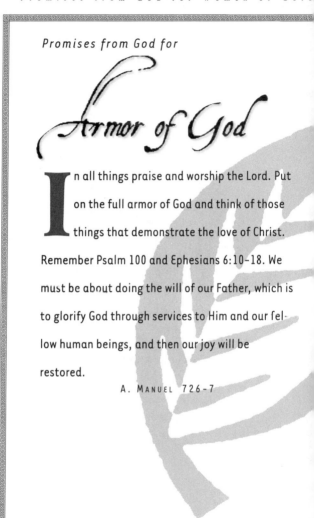

Promises from God for

Armor of God

In all things praise and worship the Lord. Put on the full armor of God and think of those things that demonstrate the love of Christ. Remember Psalm 100 and Ephesians 6:10–18. We must be about doing the will of our Father, which is to glorify God through services to Him and our fellow human beings, and then our joy will be restored.

A. MANUEL 726–7

Wherefore take unto you the whole armour of God, that ye may be able to withstand in the evil day, and having done all, to stand. Stand therefore, having your loins girt about with truth, and having on the breastplate of righteousness; And your feet shod with the preparation of the gospel of peace; Above all, taking the shield of faith, wherewith ye shall be able to quench all the fiery darts of the wicked. And take the helmet of salvation, and the sword of the Spirit, which is the word of God: Praying always with all prayer and supplication in the Spirit, and watching thereunto with all perseverance and supplication for all saints.

EPHESIANS 6:13-18

For the weapons of our warfare are not carnal, but mighty through God to the pulling down of strong holds.

2 CORINTHIANS 10:4

For the word of God is quick, and powerful, and sharper than any two-edged sword, piercing even to the dividing asunder of soul and spirit, and of the joints and marrow, and is a discerner of the thoughts and intents of the heart.

HEBREWS 4:12

Promises from God for

Belief

God's prayer promises are part of God's play to redeem all creation through the life, death, and resurrection of Jesus Christ. We are expected to pray based upon a knowledge of and belief in God's Word as revealed to us in Christ. We are to come to God in faith, believing that God is faithful to hear and answer our prayers as God's story continues to be revealed in us.

W. BULLOCK 694-23

Excerpt from the *Women of Color Study Bible*

*Call unto me, and I will answer thee,
and shew thee great and mighty things,
which thou knowest not.*

JEREMIAH 33:3

~

*Therefore I say unto you, What things soever ye
desire, when ye pray, believe that ye receive
them, and ye shall have them.*

MARK 11:24

~

*And whatsoever ye shall ask in my name, that will
I do, that the Father may be glorified in the Son.
If ye shall ask any thing in my name, I will do it.*

JOHN 14:13-14

~

*According as his divine power hath given unto us
all things that pertain unto life and godliness,
through the knowledge of him that hath called us
to glory and virtue: Whereby are given unto us
exceeding great and precious promises: that by
these ye might be partakers of the divine nature,
having escaped the corruption that
is in the world through lust.*

2 PETER 1:3-4

~

*But ye, beloved, building up yourselves on your
most holy faith, praying in the Holy Ghost.*

JUDE 1:20

Promises from God for

Commitment

s a living sacrifice our lives belong to God, and the reward becomes ours. Those who are truly committed have the full joy of knowing that they do not have to journey this life alone. Fully committed Christians benefit in a daily walk with a God who is fully committed in His endless love demonstrated in His plan of salvation.

B. WHITAKER 790-21

"MY GREAT HOPE IS TO LAUGH AS MUCH AS I CRY; TO GET MY WORK DONE AND TRY TO LOVE SOMEBODY AND HAVE THE COURAGE TO ACCEPT THE LOVE IN RETURN." **Maya Angelou, Writer**

Excerpt from the *Women of Color Study Bible*

Let your heart therefore be perfect with the Lord our God, to walk in his statutes, and to keep his commandments, as at this day.

1 KINGS 8:61

Commit thy works unto the Lord, and thy thoughts shall be established.

PROVERBS 16:3

And when he had called the people unto him with his disciples also, he said unto them, Whosoever will come after me, let him deny himself, and take up his cross, and follow me.

MARK 8:34

And whosoever doth not bear his cross, and come after me, cannot be my disciple.

LUKE 14:27

I beseech you therefore, brethren, by the mercies of God, that ye present your bodies a living sacrifice, holy, acceptable unto God, which is your reasonable service. And be not conformed to this world: but be ye transformed by the renewing of your mind, that ye may prove what is that good, and acceptable, and perfect, will of God.

ROMANS 12:1-2

Promises from God for

Confidence

The ability to enjoy life and succeed in one's pursuits is a gift from God. When we are brought into a right relationship with Him and are submissive to Him, He then gives us joy and confidence in what we do. One's confidence in oneself must be based on a solid foundation, which is God. He promises to do great things for those who wait for Him. Look to Him and persevere in hope, confidence, and patience (Isaiah 64:4).

R. HAYNES 406-14

"YOU HAVE ONLY ONE CHANCE TO MAKE A FIRST IMPRESSION. MAKE IT COUNT." **Markita Andrews, Girl Scout who holds record for cookie sales**

Excerpt from the *Women of Color Study Bible*

The Lord is my light and my salvation; whom shall I fear? the Lord is the strength of my life; of whom shall I be afraid? When the wicked, even mine enemies and my foes, came upon me to eat up my flesh, they stumbled and fell. Though an host should encamp against me, my heart shall not fear: though war should rise against me, in this will I be confident.

PSALM 27:1-3

~

And the work of righteousness shall be peace; and the effect of righteousness quietness and assurance for ever.

ISAIAH 32:17

~

Let us therefore come boldly unto the throne of grace, that we may obtain mercy, and find grace to help in time of need.

HEBREWS 4:16

~

So that we may boldly say, The Lord is my helper, and I will not fear what man shall do unto me.

HEBREWS 13:6

~

And this is the confidence that we have in him, that, if we ask any thing according to his will, he heareth us.

1 JOHN 5:14

Promises from God for

Promises from God for

Courage

It takes courage to say, "I want to be healed." Some of us have the courage to be healed. We are willing to go through the painful process of transformation. We are willing to go through the excruciating elimination of parts of ourselves in order to be fully who we were created to be. We are willing to have our wounds exposed and cleansed. We come out on the other side of pain and exposure transformed—renewed time and time again. We survive and thrive to show our daughters and sons the way through the underbrush of childhood trauma, addiction, domestic abuse, racism, sexism, oppression, neglect, and hurt.

L. LEE 150-30

Excerpt from the *Women of Color Study Bible*

For by thee I have run through a troop; and by my
God have I leaped over a wall.

PSALM 18:29

～

Wait on the Lord: be of good courage,
and he shall strengthen thine heart: wait, I say,
on the Lord.

PSALM 27:14

～

Be of good courage, and he shall strengthen your
heart, all ye that hope in the Lord.

PSALM 31:24

～

When thou passest through the waters, I will be
with thee; and through the rivers, they shall not
overflow thee: when thou walkest through the fire,
thou shalt not be burned; neither shall the flame
kindle upon thee. For I am the Lord thy God, the
Holy One of Israel, thy Saviour: I gave Egypt for
thy ransom, Ethiopia and Seba for thee.

ISAIAH 43:2-3

～

For the Lord God will help me; therefore shall I
not be confounded: therefore have I set my face
like a flint, and I know that I shall not be ashamed.

ISAIAH 50:7

Promises from God for

Discernment

he gift of discernment is best epitomized in the life of Jesus Christ. He was able to discern the thoughts and hearts of those whom He encountered (Matthew 12:25, John 6:6). The gift of discernment allows one to see beyond words and actions in order to uncover hidden motivations and intent (Proverbs 16:9). Because discernment is a gift from God, it is always subject to the written revelation of God—the Word of God.

J. THOMPSON 246-13

"IT IS NOT SO MUCH WHAT WE KNOW AS HOW WELL WE USE WHAT WE KNOW." **Ernesta Procope,**
CEO, E. G. Bowman Company

Excerpt from the *Women of Color Study Bible*

Howbeit when he, the Spirit of truth, is come, he will guide you into all truth: for he shall not speak of himself; but whatsoever he shall hear, that shall he speak: and he will shew you things to come.

JOHN 16:13

~

But the natural man receiveth not the things of the Spirit of God: for they are foolishness unto him: neither can he know them, because they are spiritually discerned. But he that is spiritual judgeth all things, yet he himself is judged of no man. For who hath known the mind of the Lord, that he may instruct him? But we have the mind of Christ.

1 CORINTHIANS 2:14-16

~

Consider what I say; and the Lord give thee understanding in all things.

2 TIMOTHY 2:7

~

Beloved, believe not every spirit, but try the spirits whether they are of God: because many false prophets are gone out into the world.

1 JOHN 4:1

~

We are of God: he that knoweth God heareth us; he that is not of God heareth not us. Hereby know we the spirit of truth, and the spirit of error.

1 JOHN 4:6

Promises from God for

Faith

God has given each person a measure of faith (Romans 12:3). It can remain stagnant or it can grow. Do nothing with faith, and even that which you have will be taken away. However, if used, like muscle, it will grow and become strong. In a world fraught with anxiety brought on by challenges, expectations, conflicts, problems, fears, strengths, hopes, and dreams, faith is essential for survival. We must posture ourselves to strengthen our faith through constantly saturating our consciousness with the Word of God until it penetrates and fills the hollow places of our souls.

C. ARCHIBALD   854-29

*Now faith is the substance of things hoped for,
the evidence of things not seen.*

HEBREWS 11:1

～

*But they that wait upon the Lord shall renew their
strength; they shall mount up with wings as eagles;
they shall run, and not be weary; and they shall
walk, and not faint.*

ISAIAH 40:31

～

*Verily, verily, I say unto you, He that believeth on
me, the works that I do shall he do also; and
greater works than these shall he do; because
I go unto my Father.*

JOHN 14:12

～

*For what saith the scripture? Abraham believed
God, and it was counted unto him for
righteousness.*

ROMANS 4:3

～

*Whom having not seen, ye love; in whom, though
now ye see him not, yet believing, ye rejoice with
joy unspeakable and full of glory.*

1 PETER 1:8

"IF YOUR FAITH CAN'T MOVE MOUNTAINS, IT SHOULD
AT LEAST CLIMB THEM." **Queen Mother Moore, Activist**

Promises from God for

Faithfulness

African-American women must abide truthfully to their positions of faithfulness as mothers, friends, and leaders. God's faithfulness toward man mirrors an example of how faithfulness leads to productivity, resulting in the fruit of diligence, security, and reliability. It also creates an atmosphere of stability—not only for self, but also for other lives as well. Our dependability and commitment to others will manifest itself in our faithfulness, love, and service to them.

T. Byrd 54-20

"THE KIND OF ANCESTORS WE HAVE IS NOT AS IMPORTANT AS THE KIND OF DESCENDANTS OUR ANCESTORS HAVE."

Phyllis A. Wallace, First African-American female to receive a Doctorate in Economics from Yale

Excerpt from the *Women of Color Study Bible*

Commit thy way unto the Lord; trust also in him; and he shall bring it to pass.

PSALM 37:5

∽

For the Lord loveth judgment, and forsaketh not his saints; they are preserved for ever: but the seed of the wicked shall be cut off.

PSALM 37:28

∽

He layeth up sound wisdom for the righteous: he is a buckler to them that walk uprightly. He keepeth the paths of judgment, and preserveth the way of his saints.

PROVERBS 2:7-8

∽

Let not mercy and truth forsake thee: bind them about thy neck; write them upon the table of thine heart: So shalt thou find favour and good understanding in the sight of God and man.

PROVERBS 3:3-4

∽

Fear none of those things which thou shalt suffer: behold, the devil shall cast some of you into prison, that ye may be tried; and ye shall have tribulation ten days: be thou faithful unto death, and I will give thee a crown of life.

REVELATION 2:10

Promises from God for

Forgiveness

To forgive is not easy, but it is possible! You must be willing to forget past hurts (Philippians 3:13), pray for the offender (1 Samuel 12:23), and give God your hurt (1 Peter 2:21-23), as well as serve as a channel for God's grace. Most importantly, we are learning that forgiveness is the doorway to reconciliation. If we desire to live reconciled lives—at peace with God and creation—we will share this gift as often as necessary. Giving it away sets us free to be healed and made whole! A forgiving spirit will bring blessings to you and others (Proverbs 11:17; 15:23).

C. BELT 694-16

For if ye forgive men their trespasses, your heavenly Father will also forgive you: But if ye forgive not men their trespasses, neither will your Father forgive your trespasses.

MATTHEW 6:14-15

~

Take heed to yourselves: If thy brother trespass against thee, rebuke him; and if he repent, forgive him. And if he trespass against thee seven times in a day, and seven times in a day turn again to thee, saying, I repent; thou shalt forgive him.

LUKE 17:3-4

~

Then came Peter to him, and said, Lord, how oft shall my brother sin against me, and I forgive him? till seven times? Jesus saith unto him, I say not unto thee, Until seven times: but, Until seventy times seven.

MATTHEW 18:21-22

~

Forbearing one another, and forgiving one another, if any man have a quarrel against any: even as Christ forgave you, so also do ye.

COLOSSIANS 3:13

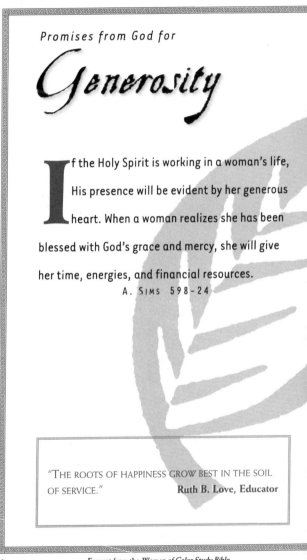

Promises from God for

Generosity

If the Holy Spirit is working in a woman's life, His presence will be evident by her generous heart. When a woman realizes she has been blessed with God's grace and mercy, she will give her time, energies, and financial resources.

A. Sims 598-24

"THE ROOTS OF HAPPINESS GROW BEST IN THE SOIL OF SERVICE." **Ruth B. Love, Educator**

The liberal soul shall be made fat: and he that
watereth shall be watered also himself.

PROVERBS 11:25

~

Give to every man that asketh of thee; and of him
that taketh away thy goods ask them not again.

LUKE 6:30

~

Give, and it shall be given unto you; good measure, pressed down, and shaken together, and run-
ning over, shall men give into your bosom. For
with the same measure that ye mete withal
it shall be measured to you again.

LUKE 6:38

~

But this I say, He which soweth sparingly shall
reap also sparingly; and he which soweth
bountifully shall reap also bountifully.
Every man according as he purposeth in his heart,
so let him give; not grudgingly, or of necessity:
for God loveth a cheerful giver.

2 CORINTHIANS 9:6-7

Promises from God for

Gentleness

entleness begins with genuine humility. Its technical meaning is "great power held in control." Being gentle is about knowing one's power, and knowing when and how to use it. Gentleness is not weakness; it is strength that is directed toward God and expressed in action with service to others. Jesus is our example of gentleness. He is the one "Who, being in the form of God, thought it not robbery to be equal with God: But made himself of no reputation, and took upon him the form of a servant, and was made in the likeness of men: And being found in fashion as a man, he humbled himself, and became obedient unto death, even the death of the cross" (Philippians 2:6-8).

C. BELT 822-30

*Take my yoke upon you, and learn of me; for I am
meek and lowly in heart: and ye shall
find rest unto your souls.*

MATTHEW 11:29

*I therefore, the prisoner of the Lord, beseech you
that ye walk worthy of the vocation wherewith ye
are called, With all lowliness and meekness, with
longsuffering, forbearing one another in love;
Endeavouring to keep the unity of the
Spirit in the bond of peace.*

EPHESIANS 4:1-3

*Whose adorning let it not be that outward adorn-
ing of plaiting the hair, and of wearing of gold, or
of putting on of apparel; But let it be the hidden
man of the heart, in that which is not corruptible,
even the ornament of a meek and quiet spirit,
which is in the sight of God of great price.*

1 PETER 3:3-4

"THE SECRET OF BEING A SAINT IS BEING A SAINT IN
SECRET." **Mary McLeod Bethune, Educator**

Promises from God for

Goodness

E ach Christian woman has a responsibility to exhibit goodness in her life. However, this goodness can only be cultivated when we abide in Jesus Christ. The Bible tells us that when we dwell in the Lord's house, goodness and mercy shall follow us all the days of our lives. When was the last time you reached out and helped another sister or brother? We live in a world where we are taught to look out for number one, to take care of our own, and to let others fend for themselves. But God calls us to another standard. We are told to maintain good works, to show a pattern of good works, and to be zealous of good works. Many persons will only see the goodness of God as they witness that goodness in us.

C. BELT 694-15

Excerpt from the *Women of Color Study Bible*

Ye are the salt of the earth: but if the salt have lost
his savour, wherewith shall it be salted? it is
thenceforth good for nothing, but to be
cast out, and to be trodden under foot of men.
Ye are the light of the world. A city that is set on
an hill cannot be hid. Neither do men light a candle,
and put it under a bushel, but on a candlestick;
and it giveth light unto all that are in the house.
Let your light so shine before men, that they may
see your good works, and glorify your Father
which is in heaven.

MATTHEW 5:13-16

And let us not be weary in well doing: for in due
season we shall reap, if we faint not.

GALATIANS 6:9

For we are his workmanship, created in Christ
Jesus unto good works, which God hath before
ordained that we should walk in them.

EPHESIANS 2:10

Beloved, follow not that which is evil, but that
which is good. He that doeth good is of God: but
he that doeth evil hath not seen God.

3 JOHN 1:11

"WHY HATE WHEN YOU COULD SPEND YOUR TIME
DOING OTHER THINGS?" **Miriam Makeba, Folksinger**

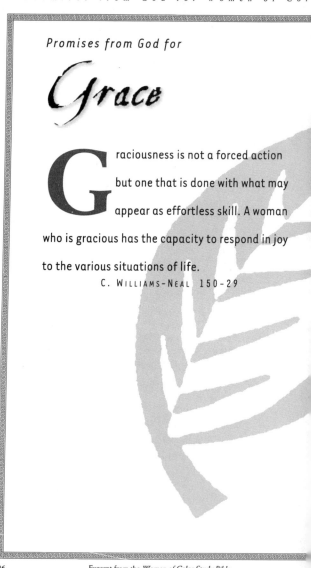

Promises from God for

Grace

G raciousness is not a forced action but one that is done with what may appear as effortless skill. A woman who is gracious has the capacity to respond in joy to the various situations of life.

C. WILLIAMS-NEAL 150-29

Excerpt from the *Women of Color Study Bible*

Gracious is the Lord, and righteous;
yea, our God is merciful.
PSALM 116:5

~

Therefore being justified by faith, we have peace
with God through our Lord Jesus Christ:
By whom also we have access by faith into this
grace wherein we stand, and rejoice
in hope of the glory of God.
ROMANS 5:1-2

~

For ye know the grace of our Lord Jesus Christ,
that, though he was rich, yet for your sakes he
became poor, that ye through his
poverty might be rich.
2 CORINTHIANS 8:9

~

And God is able to make all grace abound toward
you; that ye, always having all sufficiency in all
things, may abound to every good work.
2 CORINTHIANS 9:8

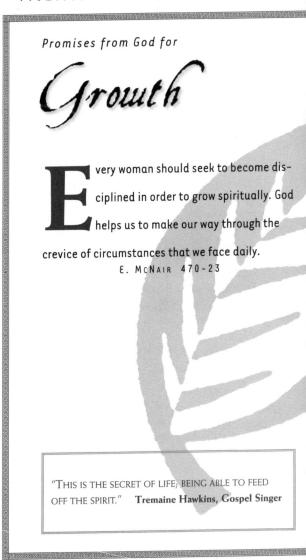

Promises from God for

Growth

Every woman should seek to become disciplined in order to grow spiritually. God helps us to make our way through the crevice of circumstances that we face daily.

E. McNair 470-23

"THIS IS THE SECRET OF LIFE; BEING ABLE TO FEED OFF THE SPIRIT." **Tremaine Hawkins, Gospel Singer**

Excerpt from the *Women of Color Study Bible*

*Thy word is a lamp unto my feet, and
a light unto my path.*

PSALM 119:105

~

*And thine ears shall hear a word behind thee,
saying, This is the way, walk ye in it, when ye turn
to the right hand, and when ye turn to the left.*

ISAIAH 30:21

~

*But the path of the just is as the shining light, that
shineth more and more unto the perfect day.*

PROVERBS 4:18

~

*And this I pray, that your love may abound yet
more and more in knowledge and in all judgment.*

PHILIPPIANS 1:9

~

*Meditate upon these things; give thyself wholly to
them; that thy profiting may appear to all.*

1 TIMOTHY 4:15

Promises from God for

Hope

But there is hope! God specializes in healing the holes in our souls and help- ing us handle life issues. Who better to heal our souls than the One who created us and gave us life? We can take comfort in knowing that God understands and God cares. The Bible teaches that we do not have a high priest that cannot be touched by the feeling of our infirmity (Hebrews 4:14-16)....Have you ever felt abandoned by God? You are not alone.

J. THOMPSON 694-21

"DISABILITIES CAN SOMETIMES BE DEFINITIONS. YOU CAN THINK OF YOURSELF IN TERMS OF WHAT YOU CAN'T DO AND NEVER REALIZE THE POSSIBILITIES OF WHAT YOU CAN DO." **Bonnie St. John, Athlete and Scholar**

The Lord taketh pleasure in them that fear him, in
those that hope in his mercy.

PSALM 147:11

∽

This I recall to my mind, therefore have I hope.
It is of the Lord's mercies that we are not consumed, because his compassions fail not.

LAMENTATIONS 3:21-22

∽

Teaching them to observe all things whatsoever I
have commanded you: and, lo, I am with you
alway, even unto the end of the world. Amen.

MATTHEW 28:20

∽

Seeing then that we have a great high priest, that
is passed into the heavens, Jesus the Son of God,
let us hold fast our profession. For we have not an
high priest which cannot be touched with the feeling of our infirmities; but was in all points tempted
like as we are, yet without sin. Let us therefore
come boldly unto the throne of grace, that we
may obtain mercy, and find grace
to help in time of need.

HEBREWS 4:14-16

∽

Let your conversation be without covetousness;
and be content with such things as ye have: for he
hath said, I will never leave thee, nor forsake thee.

HEBREWS 13:5

Promises from God for

Hope for the Future

No longer do we have to focus our attention on past failures or hurts. We can look forward with singleness of purpose. Singleness of purpose does not mean being a stranger of the covenant of promise. The promise of God's Word to women is that we will experience the fullness of His presence in our lives as we seek to know the Lord, love the Lord, and follow His Word....Attentively and purposefully, holiness drives one to the mercy of God (Luke 1:50, 58; 2 Corinthians 7:1). For it is in God's call to holiness that the believer can always find purpose.

A. HOBBS 822-23

So shall the knowledge of wisdom be unto thy soul: when thou hast found it, then there shall be a reward, and thy expectation shall not be cut off.

PROVERBS 24:14

But they that wait upon the Lord shall renew their strength; they shall mount up with wings as eagles; they shall run, and not be weary; and they shall walk, and not faint.

ISAIAH 40:31

For I know the thoughts that I think toward you, saith the Lord, thoughts of peace, and not of evil, to give you an expected end.

JEREMIAH 29:11

But ye are a chosen generation, a royal priesthood, an holy nation, a peculiar people; that ye should shew forth the praises of him who hath called you out of darkness into his marvellous light.

1 PETER 2:9

"LET A NEW EARTH RISE. LET ANOTHER WORLD BE BORN. LET A BLOODY PEACE BE WRITTEN IN THE SKY. LET A SECOND GENERATION FULL OF COURAGE ISSUE FORTH. LET A PEOPLE LOVING FREEDOM COME TO GROWTH." **Margaret Walker, Researcher and Lecturer**

Promises from God for

Joy

True joy is evident regardless of circumstances. Those who love God rejoice even in the midst of troubles (James 1:2-3). There were times when heaven itself looked down and wondered at the joy and adulation of God's children. This joy expressed itself most often when the slaves gathered in brush arbors, in fields, and in secret places for worship. That's the key to joy: giving honor to the most high God. Communion with God produces joy—joy like a river, joy unspeakable, joy flooding the soul!

C. BELT 406-12

"THERE'S A FRESHNESS AND UNIQUENESS ABOUT DANCE BECAUSE IT CONSTANTLY CHANGES. VARIETY IS THE SPICE OF LIFE." **Judith Jamison, Director, Alvin Ailey Dance Theater**

*But let all those that put their trust in thee rejoice:
let them ever shout for joy, because thou
defendest them: let them also that love thy
name be joyful in thee.*

PSALM 5:11

~

*Be glad in the Lord, and rejoice, ye righteous: and
shout for joy, all ye that are upright in heart.*

PSALM 32:11

~

*Thou hast turned for me my mourning into danc-
ing: thou hast put off my sackcloth, and girded me
with gladness; To the end that my glory may sing
praise to thee, and not be silent. O Lord my God,
I will give thanks unto thee for ever.*

PSALM 30:11-12

~

*For thou, Lord, hast made me glad through thy
work: I will triumph in the works of thy hands.*

PSALM 92:4

~

*My brethren, count it all joy when ye fall into
divers temptations; Knowing this, that the
trying of your faith worketh patience.*

JAMES 1:2-3

Promises from God for

Kindness

Kindness is treating others with love and respect. Kindness in the Old and New Testaments refers to love that is expressed in actions. Kindness is not a natural human trait. It must be developed in women to enable us to express that kindness to others in the name of God. Since God has been kind to us, we as God's children should show kindness to others even in the midst of conflict. Over and over again the Bible tells us that we must be kind to those who are poor and oppressed....Often the kindness that we extend to others goes unnoticed. But we must always remember that God notices. My sisters, "Be not weary in well doing" (2 Thessalonians 3:13). The kindness that God shows to His children is everlasting.

C. BELT 406-14

Excerpt from the *Women of Color Study Bible*

*A gracious woman retaineth honour: and
strong men retain riches.*
PROVERBS 11:16

~

*He that oppresseth the poor reproacheth his
Maker: but he that honoureth him hath
mercy on the poor.*
PROVERBS 14:31

~

*Therefore all things whatsoever ye would that
men should do to you, do ye even so to them:
for this is the law and the prophets.*
MATTHEW 7:12

~

*See that none render evil for evil unto any man;
but ever follow that which is good, both
among yourselves, and to all men.*
1 THESSALONIANS 5:15

~

*And beside this, giving all diligence, add to your
faith virtue; and to virtue knowledge; And to knowledge temperance; and to temperance patience; and
to patience godliness; And to godliness brotherly
kindness; and to brotherly kindness charity.*
2 PETER 1:5-7

"WHAT YOU OUGHT TO DO, YOU SHOULD DO; AND
WHAT YOU SHOULD DO, YOU OUGHT TO DO!"
Oprah Winfrey, Talk-Show Host

Promises from God for

Knowing God

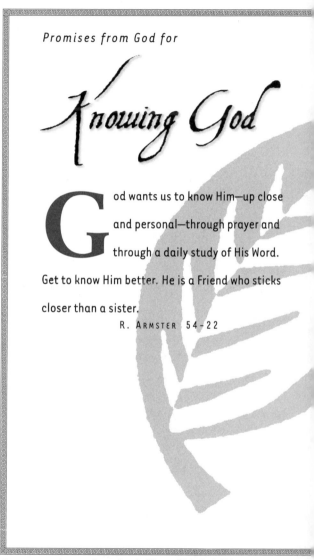

God wants us to know Him—up close and personal—through prayer and through a daily study of His Word. Get to know Him better. He is a Friend who sticks closer than a sister.

R. ARMSTER 54-22

Excerpt from the *Women of Color Study Bible*

And thou shalt love the Lord thy God with
all thine heart, and with all thy soul, and
with all thy might.

DEUTERONOMY 6:5

～

Thou wilt shew me the path of life: in thy presence is fulness of joy; at thy right hand there
are pleasures for evermore.

PSALM 16:11

～

Behold, the eye of the Lord is upon them that fear
him, upon them that hope in his mercy.

PSALM 33:18

～

The eyes of the Lord are upon the righteous, and
his ears are open unto their cry.

PSALM 34:15

～

Being confident of this very thing, that he which
hath begun a good work in you will perform it
until the day of Jesus Christ.

PHILIPPIANS. 1:6

Promises from God for

Leadership

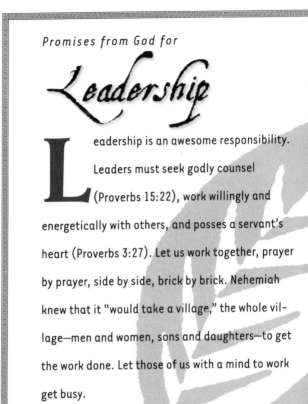

Leadership is an awesome responsibility. Leaders must seek godly counsel (Proverbs 15:22), work willingly and energetically with others, and posses a servant's heart (Proverbs 3:27). Let us work together, prayer by prayer, side by side, brick by brick. Nehemiah knew that it "would take a village," the whole village—men and women, sons and daughters—to get the work done. Let those of us with a mind to work get busy.

D. JOHNSON 374-8

"BLACK WOMEN ARE NOT HERE TO COMPETE OR
FIGHT WITH YOU, BROTHERS. IF WE HAVE HANG-UPS
ABOUT BEING MALE OR FEMALE, WE'RE NOT GOING
TO BE ABLE TO USE OUR TALENTS TO LIBERATE ALL OF
OUR BLACK PEOPLE."   **Shirley Chisholm,
Former Congresswoman**

*Withhold not good from them to whom it is due,
when it is in the power of thine hand to do it.*
PROVERBS 3:27

*Without counsel purposes are disappointed: but in
the multitude of counsellors they are established.*
PROVERBS 15:22

*So likewise ye, when ye shall have done all those
things which are commanded you, say,
We are unprofitable servants: we have done that
which was our duty to do.*
LUKE 17:10

*With good will doing service, as to the
Lord, and not to men.*
EPHESIANS 6:7

*If any man speak, let him speak as the oracles of
God; if any man minister, let him do it as of the
ability which God giveth: that God in all things
may be glorified through Jesus Christ, to whom be
praise and dominion for ever and ever. Amen.*
1 PETER 4:11

Promises from God for

$\mathcal{L}$ove

As we look at the challenges facing the black community, we must understand that love is the only power that will save us. God's love can look at the worst situation and see hope. God's love can stand in the midst of hate and poverty and speak a word of deliverance. God's love can transform communities and transform minds. "The fruit of the Spirit is love . . . against such there is no law" (Galatians 5:22-23).

C. BELT 822-25

"I LEAVE YOU LOVE. LOVE BUILDS. IT IS POSITIVE AND HELPFUL. IT IS MORE BENEFICIAL THAN HATE. INJURIES QUICKLY FORGOTTEN QUICKLY PASS AWAY. PERSONALLY AND RADICALLY, OUR ENEMIES MUST BE FORGIVEN." **Mary McLeod Bethune, Educator**

Excerpt from the *Women of Color Study Bible*

Oh that men would praise the Lord for his goodness, and for his wonderful works to the children of men! For he satisfieth the longing soul, and filleth the hungry soul with goodness.

PSALM 107:8-9

~

The Lord is gracious, and full of compassion; slow to anger, and of great mercy.

PSALM 145:8

~

For the mountains shall depart, and the hills be removed; but my kindness shall not depart from thee, neither shall the covenant of my peace be removed, saith the Lord that hath mercy on thee.

ISAIAH 54:10

~

The Lord hath appeared of old unto me, saying, Yea, I have loved thee with an everlasting love: therefore with lovingkindness have I drawn thee.

JEREMIAH 31:3

~

Charity suffereth long, and is kind; charity envieth not; charity vaunteth not itself, is not puffed up, Doth not behave itself unseemly, seeketh not her own, is not easily provoked, thinketh no evil; Rejoiceth not in iniquity, but rejoiceth in the truth; Beareth all things, believeth all things, hopeth all things, endureth all things.

1 CORINTHIANS 13:4-7

Promises from God for

Patience

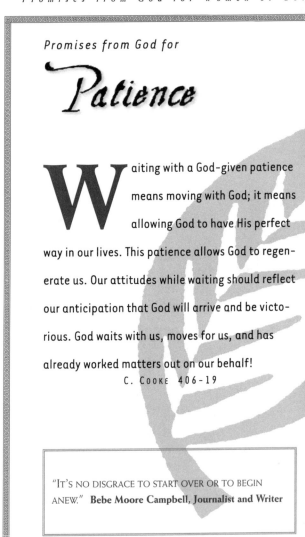

Waiting with a God-given patience means moving with God; it means allowing God to have His perfect way in our lives. This patience allows God to regenerate us. Our attitudes while waiting should reflect our anticipation that God will arrive and be victorious. God waits with us, moves for us, and has already worked matters out on our behalf!

C. COOKE 406-19

"IT'S NO DISGRACE TO START OVER OR TO BEGIN ANEW." **Bebe Moore Campbell, Journalist and Writer**

Rest in the Lord, and wait patiently for him: fret not thyself because of him who prospereth in his way, because of the man who bringeth wicked devices to pass.

PSALM 37:7

~

But thou, O Lord, art a God full of compassion, and gracious, longsuffering, and plenteous in mercy and truth.

PSALM 86:15

~

I wait for the Lord, my soul doth wait, and in his word do I hope. My soul waiteth for the Lord more than they that watch for the morning: I say, more than they that watch for the morning.

PSALM 130:5-6

~

And not only so, but we glory in tribulations also: knowing that tribulation worketh patience; And patience, experience; and experience, hope: And hope maketh not ashamed; because the love of God is shed abroad in our hearts by the Holy Ghost which is given unto us.

ROMANS 5:3-5

~

But the fruit of the Spirit is love, joy, peace, long-suffering, gentleness, goodness, faith, Meekness, temperance: against such there is no law.

GALATIANS 5:22-23

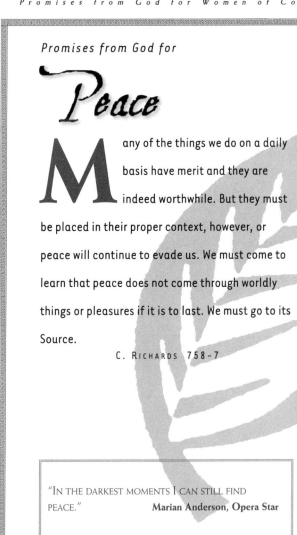

Promises from God for

Peace

Many of the things we do on a daily basis have merit and they are indeed worthwhile. But they must be placed in their proper context, however, or peace will continue to evade us. We must come to learn that peace does not come through worldly things or pleasures if it is to last. We must go to its Source.

C. RICHARDS 758-7

"IN THE DARKEST MOMENTS I CAN STILL FIND PEACE." **Marian Anderson, Opera Star**

Excerpt from the *Women of Color Study Bible*

Great peace have they which love thy law: and nothing shall offend them.

PSALM 119:165

~

Thou wilt keep him in perfect peace, whose mind is stayed on thee: because he trusteth in thee.

ISAIAH 26:3

~

For to be carnally minded is death; but to be spiritually minded is life and peace.

ROMANS 8:6

~

Peace I leave with you, my peace I give unto you: not as the world giveth, give I unto you. Let not your heart be troubled, neither let it be afraid.

JOHN 14:27

~

And the peace of God, which passeth all understanding, shall keep your hearts and minds through Christ Jesus.

PHILIPPIANS 4:7

Promises from God for

Perseverance

omen today must still heed the call of the Lord and submit their bodies as vessels to bring forth God's Word, life, and presence. As long as God's promises are "Yea" and "Amen," truth and completion, reality and fulfillment, women must look to Him in faith, humble themselves, pray, seek God's will for their lives, and cease from doing evil.

M. V. STEPHENS 726-5

"YOU DON'T MAKE PROGRESS BY STANDING ON THE SIDELINES, WHIMPERING AND COMPLAINING. YOU MAKE PROGRESS BY IMPLEMENTING IDEAS."

Shirley Chisholm, Former Congresswoman

*Hold up my goings in thy paths, that my
footsteps slip not.*
PSALM 17:5

～

*To them who by patient continuance in well
doing seek for glory and honour and
immortality, eternal life.*
ROMANS 2:7

～

*And let us not be weary in well doing: for in due
season we shall reap, if we faint not.*
GALATIANS 6:9

～

*But let patience have her perfect work, that ye
may be perfect and entire, wanting nothing.
If any of you lack wisdom, let him ask of God, that
giveth to all men liberally, and upbraideth not;
and it shall be given him.*
JAMES 1:4-5

～

*For all the promises of God in him are yea, and in
him Amen, unto the glory of God by us.*
2 CORINTHIANS 1:20

Promises from God for

Prayer

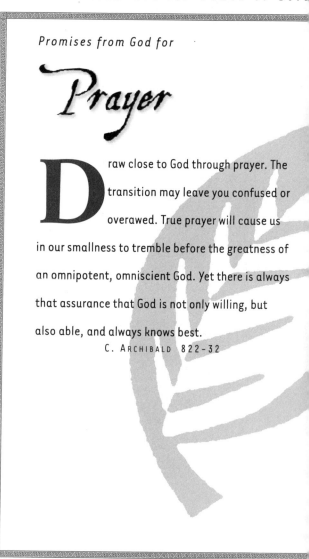

Draw close to God through prayer. The transition may leave you confused or overawed. True prayer will cause us in our smallness to tremble before the greatness of an omnipotent, omniscient God. Yet there is always that assurance that God is not only willing, but also able, and always knows best.

C. ARCHIBALD 822-32

*Come unto me, all ye that labour and are heavy
laden, and I will give you rest. Take my yoke
upon you, and learn of me; for I am meek
and lowly in heart: and ye shall find rest
unto your souls. For my yoke is easy,
and my burden is light.*

MATTHEW 11:28-30

∾

*Watch and pray, that ye enter not into
temptation: the spirit indeed is willing,
but the flesh is weak.*

MATTHEW 26:41

∾

*Praying always with all prayer and supplication in
the Spirit, and watching thereunto with all perseverance and supplication for all saints.*

EPHESIANS 6:18

∾

*Continue in prayer, and watch in the
same with thanksgiving.*

COLOSSIANS 4:2

∾

*Rejoice evermore. Pray without ceasing.
In every thing give thanks: for this is the will of
God in Christ Jesus concerning you.*

1 THESSALONIANS 5:16-18

Promises from God for

Prayer Life

Begin to pray for provision by starting with a plan. First, stop worrying and start praying (Psalm 37:1-6). Second, with prayers, supplication, thanksgiving, let your request be made known to God (Philippians 4:6). Next, reflect and examine your circumstances and find contentment. Things might not be as bad as you thought (Philippians 4:9-13). Observe how other Christian women found favor through prayers (2 Kings 4:1-7; Matthew 9:20-22). Then give yourself permission to ask and seek a solution. If a child or a friend comes to you and asks for bread would you give them a stone? No! God also gives what is good unto those that ask (Matthew 7:7-11). Finally, renew your faith, release your fears (Hebrews 12:1-3), and believe (Matthew 9:23; 21:21-22; Mark 9:23; John 20:25).

N. PEETE 694-17

Excerpt from the *Women of Color Study Bible*

*In my distress I called upon the Lord, and cried
unto my God: he heard my voice out of his temple,
and my cry came before him, even into his ears.*

PSALM 18:6

*Jesus answered and said unto them, Verily I say
unto you, If ye have faith, and doubt not, ye shall
not only do this which is done to the fig tree, but
also if ye shall say unto this mountain, Be thou
removed, and be thou cast into the sea; it shall be
done. And all things, whatsoever ye shall ask in
prayer, believing, ye shall receive.*

MATTHEW 21:21-22

*Be careful for nothing; but in every thing by
prayer and supplication with thanksgiving let your
requests be made known unto God.*

PHILIPPIANS. 4:6

*But my God shall supply all your need according
to his riches in glory by Christ Jesus.*

PHILIPPIANS. 4:19

Promises from God for

Purpose

Whether we are in the race toward a good marriage, financial stability, a college degree, certification, or other challenges, we must persevere. Life's victories are not won by those with the best plans but by those who, through faith, persevere in the race. If you stay focused on Jesus you can hold up under any load.

In life, if you have a purpose in which you can believe, there's no end to the amount of things you can accomplish. —MARIAN ANDERSON

C. GRACE-SCOTT 854-30

"I'M NO MARTYR. I JUST HAD A HARD DAY AT WORK. MY FEET WERE HURTING, AND I WAS TOO TIRED TO GIVE UP MY SEAT." **Rosa Parks, Mother of the Civil Rights Movement**

Excerpt from the *Women of Color Study Bible*

*But seek ye first the kingdom of God, and his
righteousness; and all these things shall
be added unto you.*

MATTHEW 6:33

~

*But he that shall endure unto the end, the
same shall be saved.*

MATTHEW 24:13

~

*For our light affliction, which is but for a moment,
worketh for us a far more exceeding and eternal
weight of glory.*

2 CORINTHIANS 4:17

~

*Blessed is the man that endureth temptation: for
when he is tried, he shall receive the crown
of life, which the Lord hath promised
to them that love him.*

JAMES 1:12

~

*Wherefore seeing we also are compassed about
with so great a cloud of witnesses, let us lay aside
every weight, and the sin which doth so easily
beset us, and let us run with patience the
race that is set before us.*

HEBREWS 12:1

Promises from God for

Reliance

T hen one day, she stumbles upon Romans 7:15-25. It is then that she begins to understand what every truly strong Black woman knows: an admission of personal powerlessness is a willingness to rely on the One who has all power. From this moment on, she begins to be open to God for direction in obtaining the medical, emotional, and spiritual help needed for a recovery with dignity for a strong Black woman.

L. J. HOOD 790-19

Excerpt from the *Women of Color Study Bible*

*I will seek that which was lost, and bring again that
which was driven away, and will bind up that
which was broken, and will strengthen
that which was sick: but I will destroy the fat and
the strong; I will feed them with judgment.*

EZEKIEL 34:16

*Therefore if any man be in Christ, he is a new
creature: old things are passed away; behold, all
things are become new. And all things are of God,
who hath reconciled us to himself by Jesus Christ,
and hath given to us the ministry of
reconciliation.*

2 CORINTHIANS 5:17-18

*But the God of all grace, who hath called us unto
his eternal glory by Christ Jesus, after that ye have
suffered a while, make you perfect, stablish,
strengthen, settle you.*

1 PETER 5:10

*O wretched man that I am! who shall deliver me
from the body of this death? I thank God through
Jesus Christ our Lord. So then with the mind I
myself serve the law of God; but with the
flesh the law of sin.*

ROMANS 7:24-25

Promises from God for

Salvation

S alvation is all-encompassing. It is our healing, our preservation, our protection, our welfare, our deliverance, our health, our help. God, in His infinite wisdom and power and mercy, knew that we needed to be saved from sickness, disease, calamity, bondage, and the ultimate—eternal death. Christ came and saved us from everything that is ungodly, everything that is not like Him. This is our salvation. Jesus, Hebrew for Joshua or yeshua, means "salvation." He is our salvation.

C. BYRD 790-19

That if thou shalt confess with thy mouth the
Lord Jesus, and shalt believe in thine heart that
God hath raised him from the dead, thou shalt be
saved. For with the heart man believeth unto
righteousness; and with the mouth confession is
made unto salvation.

ROMANS 10:9-10

❦

He brought me up also out of an horrible pit, out
of the miry clay, and set my feet upon a rock,
and established my goings.

PSALM 40:2

❦

For all have sinned, and come short
of the glory of God.

ROMANS 3:23

❦

For this is good and acceptable in the
sight of God our Saviour;
Who will have all men to be saved, and
to come unto the knowledge of the truth.

1 TIMOTHY 2:3-4

❦

Not by works of righteousness which we have
done, but according to his mercy he saved us, by
the washing of regeneration, and renewing
of the Holy Ghost.

TITUS 3:5

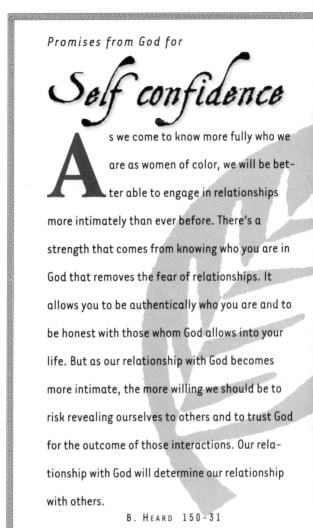

Promises from God for

Self confidence

As we come to know more fully who we are as women of color, we will be better able to engage in relationships more intimately than ever before. There's a strength that comes from knowing who you are in God that removes the fear of relationships. It allows you to be authentically who you are and to be honest with those whom God allows into your life. But as our relationship with God becomes more intimate, the more willing we should be to risk revealing ourselves to others and to trust God for the outcome of those interactions. Our relationship with God will determine our relationship with others.

B. HEARD 150-31

Excerpt from the *Women of Color Study Bible*

Know ye that the Lord he is God: it is he that
hath made us, and not we ourselves; we are his
people, and the sheep of his pasture.

PSALM 100:3

Can a woman forget her sucking child, that she
should not have compassion on the son of her
womb? yea, they may forget, yet will I not forget
thee. Behold, I have graven thee upon the palms
of my hands; thy walls are continually before me.

ISAIAH 49:15-16

The Lord hath appeared of old unto me, saying,
Yea, I have loved thee with an everlasting love:
therefore with lovingkindness have I drawn thee.

JEREMIAH 31:3

Are not two sparrows sold for a farthing? and one
of them shall not fall on the ground without your
Father. But the very hairs of your head are all
numbered. Fear ye not therefore, ye are of
more value than many sparrows.

MATTHEW 10:29-31

"I'VE MADE MISTAKES; WE ALL DO. BUT I DON'T
BELIEVE THAT YOU HAVE TO HAVE DONE IT BEFORE
TO DO IT WELL. YOU ONLY HAVE TO BE SMART AND
TALENTED TO DO IT WELL." **Suzanne De Passe,
President, Gordy/De Passe Productions**

Promises from God for

Self control

As a young African-American woman, I know that in order to stay in control I must study God's Word and allow it to sink into my heart. I know that self-control is necessary for my personal development, my spiritual growth, and my Christian service. Sometimes that is hard, especially when many of my friends try to put me down. I believe that my generation is called for a special purpose in God. When we live our lives with self-control, we acknowledge that God has a plan for our lives; thus, we tell the world that we have chosen to honor God's purpose. Without self-control, we have little opportunity to experience God's blessings.

K. BELT 854-29

Let the words of my mouth, and the meditation of my heart, be acceptable in thy sight, O Lord, my strength, and my redeemer.

PSALM 19:14

❧

But the fruit of the Spirit is love, joy, peace, longsuffering, gentleness, goodness, faith, Meekness, temperance: against such there is no law.

GALATIANS 5:22-23

❧

But refuse profane and old wives' fables, and exercise thyself rather unto godliness. For bodily exercise profiteth little: but godliness is profitable unto all things, having promise of the life that now is, and of that which is to come.

1 TIMOTHY 4:7-8

❧

That they may teach the young women to be sober, to love their husbands, to love their children, To be discreet, chaste, keepers at home, good, obedient to their own husbands, that the word of God be not blasphemed.

TITUS 2:4-5

Promises from God for

Serving

African-American women have a unique opportunity to illustrate to the remainder of the body of Christ and the world: the godly principle of denying oneself and living for Christ and others (John 15:12-17). This is the legacy of our foreparents—a legacy not of gold, silver, and worldly riches, but one of sacrifice, service, and love for Christ and the body of Christ (John 12:25-26; Romans 12:10; 1 Corinthians 13:1-3). We must again remove ourselves from the standards of success set by the world and look to the Word of God for our validation (John 6:27; Romans 12:1-2).

A. MANUEL 758-8

> "OUR AIM SHOULD BE SERVICE, NOT SUCCESS."
> **Barbara Smith, Former Model and Restaurateur**

Excerpt from the *Women of Color Study Bible*

So likewise ye, when ye shall have done all those things which are commanded you, say, We are unprofitable servants: we have done that which was our duty to do.

LUKE 17:10

~

This is my commandment, That ye love one another, as I have loved you. Greater love hath no man than this, that a man lay down his life for his friends. Ye are my friends, if ye do whatsoever I command you. Henceforth I call you not servants; for the servant knoweth not what his lord doeth: but I have called you friends; for all things that I have heard of my Father I have made known unto you.

JOHN 15:12-15

~

Hereby perceive we the love of God, because he laid down his life for us: and we ought to lay down our lives for the brethren. But whoso hath this world's good, and seeth his brother have need, and shutteth up his bowels of compassion from him, how dwelleth the love of God in him?

1 JOHN 3:16-17

Promises from God for

Suffering

The thread that maintains a sense of balance between life and suffering is our faith. Faith becomes the hinge to the door of life, or the vein that carries life to the soul. Our suffering comes as a test of our profession of faith in God through Christ Jesus. It comes as a unique opportunity to glorify God. Our suffering is our testament that "neither death, nor life, nor angels, nor principalities, nor powers, nor things present, nor things to come, nor height, nor depth, nor any other creature, shall be able to separate us from the love of God, which is in Christ Jesus our Lord" (Romans 8:38-39).

L. WOODEN   694-19

Excerpt from the *Women of Color Study Bible*

*But we have this treasure in earthen vessels, that
the excellency of the power may be of God, and
not of us. We are troubled on every side, yet not
distressed; we are perplexed, but not in despair;
Persecuted, but not forsaken; cast down,
but not destroyed.*

2 CORINTHIANS 4:7-9

~

*Let thy mercy, O Lord, be upon us, according
as we hope in thee.*

PSALM 33:22

~

*And Jesus said unto them, Because of your unbe-
lief: for verily I say unto you, If ye have faith as a
grain of mustard seed, ye shall say unto this mountain, Remove hence to yonder place; and it shall
remove; and nothing shall be impossible unto you.*

MATTHEW 17:20

~

*Therefore being justified by faith, we have peace
with God through our Lord Jesus Christ.*

ROMANS 5:1

~

*Who by him do believe in God, that raised him up
from the dead, and gave him glory; that your faith
and hope might be in God.*

1 PETER 1:21

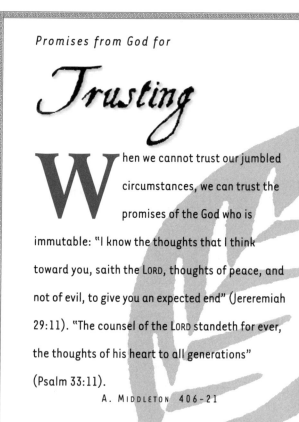

Promises from God for

Trusting

When we cannot trust our jumbled circumstances, we can trust the promises of the God who is immutable: "I know the thoughts that I think toward you, saith the LORD, thoughts of peace, and not of evil, to give you an expected end" (Jereremiah 29:11). "The counsel of the LORD standeth for ever, the thoughts of his heart to all generations" (Psalm 33:11).

A. MIDDLETON 406-21

"I WOULD FIGHT FOR MY LIBERTY SO LONG AS MY STRENGTH LASTED, AND IF THE TIME CAME FOR ME TO GO, THE LORD WOULD LET THEM TAKE ME."
Harriet Tubman, Underground Railroad Conductor

But thou art the same, and thy years shall have no end. The children of thy servants shall continue, and their seed shall be established before thee.

PSALM 102:27-28

～

It is better to trust in the Lord than to put confidence in man.

PSALM 118:8

～

Thou wilt keep him in perfect peace, whose mind is stayed on thee: because he trusteth in thee. Trust ye in the Lord for ever: for in the Lord Jehovah is everlasting strength:

ISAIAH 26:3-4

～

For thus saith the Lord God, the Holy One of Israel; In returning and rest shall ye be saved; in quietness and in confidence shall be your strength: and ye would not.

ISAIAH 30:15

～

Blessed is the man that trusteth in the Lord, and whose hope the Lord is. For he shall be as a tree planted by the waters, and that spreadeth out her roots by the river, and shall not see when heat cometh, but her leaf shall be green; and shall not be careful in the year of drought, neither shall cease from yielding fruit.

JEREMIAH 17:7-8

Promises from God for

Witnessing

Today, the harvest is plentiful. It is the laborers that are few. Could it be because we have not utilized the resources we have in our own backyard? When was the last time you went fishing for Christ?...When was the last time you baited your rod? Or has your rod, your reel, your pole simply gathered cobwebs in your shed? Is it because your net is broken? Is it because you're out of practice? Is it because you're out of bait? Well, Jesus said, "If you will simply lift me up before men, I'll do the drawing!" (paraphrased). Let me take this time out to remind you that if you give one a fish, you supply her with a meal, but if you teach her to fish, you equip her for life—both practically and spiritually.

L. MELTON-DOLBERRY 694-22

Excerpt from the *Women of Color Study Bible*

He that goeth forth and weepeth, bearing precious seed, shall doubtless come again with rejoicing, bringing his sheaves with him.

PSALM 126:6

And Jesus came and spake unto them, saying, All power is given unto me in heaven and in earth. Go ye therefore, and teach all nations, baptizing them in the name of the Father, and of the Son, and of the Holy Ghost: Teaching them to observe all things whatsoever I have commanded you: and, lo, I am with you alway, even unto the end of the world. Amen.

MATTHEW 28:18-20

Therefore said he unto them, The harvest truly is great, but the labourers are few: pray ye therefore the Lord of the harvest, that he would send forth labourers into his harvest.

LUKE 10:2

And many of the Samaritans of that city believed on him for the saying of the woman, which testified, He told me all that ever I did.

JOHN 4:39

"PEOPLE MAY DOUBT WHAT YOU SAY, BUT THEY WILL ALWAYS BELIEVE WHAT YOU DO." **Nannie Helen Burroughs, Educator and Civil Rights Activist**

*Family
Issues*

Promises from God for

Children

The Bible teaches us that children are entitled to be respected for their childlike opinions. God teaches us when to use the rod and when to listen to correct unacceptable behavior. Correcting bad behavior promptly will prevent unacceptable patterns from being established. Discipline helps the child to understand that he or she not only disobeyed his/her parents, but God as well.

F. Johnson 470-20

"WE WANTED SOMETHING FOR OURSELVES AND FOR OUR CHILDREN, SO WE TOOK A CHANCE WITH OUR LIVES." **Unita Blackwell, Civil Rights Activist; First African-American Mayor in Mississippi**

Honour thy father and thy mother: that thy days may be long upon the land which the Lord thy God giveth thee.

EXODUS 20:12

Train up a child in the way he should go: and when he is old, he will not depart from it.

PROVERBS 22:6

For they verily for a few days chastened us after their own pleasure; but he for our profit, that we might be partakers of his holiness. Now no chastening for the present seemeth to be joyous, but grievous: nevertheless afterward it yieldeth the peaceable fruit of righteousness unto them which are exercised thereby.

HEBREWS 12:10-11

Chasten thy son while there is hope, and let not thy soul spare for his crying.

PROVERBS 19:18

The rod and reproof give wisdom: but a child left to himself bringeth his mother to shame.

PROVERBS 29:15

Promises from God for

Discipline

A Spirit-led mother understands that in the midst of a disciplinary act, she must always show the kind of love that God shows when He disciplines us. Like our mothers would tell us, sometimes "It really does hurt me more than it does you!" Peace of mind will come through the foundational love God requires in the obedience to His Word.

A. FOSTER 278-15

Excerpt from the *Women of Color Study Bible*

Thou shalt also consider in thine heart, that, as a man chasteneth his son, so the Lord thy God chasteneth thee.

DEUTERONOMY 8:5

Even a child is known by his doings, whether his work be pure, and whether it be right.

PROVERBS 20:11

Correct thy son, and he shall give thee rest; yea, he shall give delight unto thy soul.

PROVERBS 29:17

He that spareth his rod hateth his son: but he that loveth him chasteneth him betimes.

PROVERBS 13:24

I have no greater joy than to hear that my children walk in truth.

3 JOHN 1:4

Promises from God for

Gift of Children

Throughout the African-American culture, children have been valued. To assure their children's rightful place in society and in the kingdom of God, parents must introduce them to Jesus. Children must be prepared to fulfill God's call (1 Chronicles 22:7-10), encouraged to follow wisdom (Proverbs 4:3-4), taught to make their own choices (Proverbs 22:6), and instructed to obey their parents in the Lord (Ephesians 6:1, 4)....To build meaningful relationships with children, parents should provide a living environment that is filled with encouragement and spoken love. Our children will then "build" strong, godly sons and daughters into the generations. African-American children are a blessed heritage from God.

G. LONDON 694-23

*Lo, children are an heritage of the Lord: and the
fruit of the womb is his reward. As arrows are in
the hand of a mighty man; so are children of the
youth. Happy is the man that hath his quiver full
of them: they shall not be ashamed, but they shall
speak with the enemies in the gate.*

PSALM 127:3-5

*And whosoever shall give to drink unto one of
these little ones a cup of cold water only in the
name of a disciple, verily I say unto you, he shall
in no wise lose his reward.*

MATTHEW 10:42

*But when Jesus saw it, he was much displeased,
and said unto them, Suffer the little children to
come unto me, and forbid them not: for of such is
the kingdom of God. Verily I say unto you,
Whosoever shall not receive the kingdom of God
as a little child, he shall not enter therein.
And he took them up in his arms, put his hands
upon them, and blessed them.*

MARK 10:14-16

"IF YOU CAN'T HOLD CHILDREN IN YOUR ARMS,
PLEASE HOLD THEM IN YOUR HEART."

Clara "Mother" Hale, Founder, The Hale House

Promises from God for

God as example

God is our example of a loving parent. Parenting is praising, advising, reminding, encouraging, nurturing, teaching/training (Psalm 78:1-8; Proverbs 22:6; 2 Timothy 1:3-5); influencing, nourishing, giving, and disciplining children (Proverbs 13:24; Hebrews 12:5-8). It is teaching them to live a Christian life by word and example. Parenting requires patience and compassion. You have to mirror the attributes of God (persistence, patience, mercy) and demonstrate a good Christian marriage (1 Timothy 3:4, 12). It helps if you are reliable and trustworthy, like God. Your children depend on you to be there for them.

S. DEMBY 854-28

Excerpt from the *Women of Color Study Bible*

Hear, O Israel: The Lord our God is one Lord:
And thou shalt love the Lord thy God with all
thine heart, and with all thy soul, and with all thy
might. And these words, which I command thee
this day, shall be in thine heart: And thou shalt
teach them diligently unto thy children, and shalt
talk of them when thou sittest in thine house, and
when thou walkest by the way, and when thou
liest down, and when thou risest up.

DEUTERONOMY 6:4-7

Chasten thy son while there is hope, and let not
thy soul spare for his crying.

PROVERBS 19:18

Train up a child in the way he should go: and
when he is old, he will not depart from it.

PROVERBS 22:6

And will be a Father unto you, and ye shall be my
sons and daughters, saith the Lord Almighty.

2 CORINTHIANS 6:18

Promises from God for

Marriage

The greatest example of marital intimacy in Scripture is the beautiful Song of Solomon, a story of the love between a king and a young maiden. It paints a picture of mutual devotion and adoration. It portrays two who delight in each other to the exclusion of all others (Song of Solomon 7:10). Though it exalts physical beauty and intimacy (Song of Solomon 4:1-15; 6:4-7; 7:17), it also speaks of the spiritual dimension of genuine love as emanating from the soul, or very core of our being (3:4). Such love, it says, is better "than wine" (4:10) and "strong as death" (8:6).

E. ALEXANDER 246-11

For this cause shall a man leave his father and
mother, and shall be joined unto his wife, and they
two shall be one flesh. This is a great mystery: but
I speak concerning Christ and the church.
Nevertheless let every one of you in particular so
love his wife even as himself; and the wife see that
she reverence her husband.

EPHESIANS 5:31-33

And they twain shall be one flesh:
so then they are no more twain, but one flesh.
What therefore God hath joined together,
let not man put asunder.

MARK 10:8-9

The wife hath not power of her own body, but the
husband: and likewise also the husband hath not
power of his own body, but the wife.

1 CORINTHIANS 7:4

"THE DIVORCE RATE WOULD BE LOWER IF, INSTEAD
OF MARRYING FOR BETTER OR WORSE, PEOPLE WOULD
MARRY FOR GOOD." **Ruby Dee, Actress**

Promises from God for

Motherhood

In the forty-ninth chapter of Isaiah, the prophet uses an illustration of a newborn baby's mother to remind us that God's love for His people is unchanging. Isaiah reminds us that the love we have for those entrusted to our mothering care is like the sacrificial love God has for us. Because there is not a circumstance that can separate us from God's love, we ought not to allow anything to separate us from our love for our beloved. One that loves as God loves will correct and punish for the good of her beloved one's eternal destiny (Deuteronomy 8:5).

A. FOSTER 278-15

Thou shalt also consider in thine heart, that, as a
man chasteneth his son, so the Lord thy God
chasteneth thee.

DEUTERONOMY 8:5

~

Every wise woman buildeth her house: but the
foolish plucketh it down with her hands.

PROVERBS 14:1

~

For thus saith the Lord, Behold, I will extend
peace to her like a river, and the glory of the
Gentiles like a flowing stream: then shall ye suck,
ye shall be borne upon her sides, and be dandled
upon her knees. As one whom his mother comforteth, so will I comfort you; and ye shall be
comforted in Jerusalem.

ISAIAH 66:12-13

~

O Jerusalem, Jerusalem, which killest the
prophets, and stonest them that are sent unto
thee; how often would I have gathered thy
children together, as a hen doth gather her brood
under her wings, and ye would not!

LUKE 13:34

"I HAD...FOUND THAT MOTHERHOOD WAS A PROFES-
SION BY ITSELF, JUST LIKE SCHOOL TEACHING AND
LECTURING..." **Ida B. Wells-Barnett,
Teacher and Journalist**

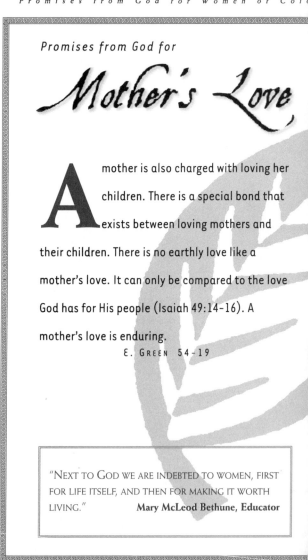

Promises from God for

Mother's Love

A mother is also charged with loving her children. There is a special bond that exists between loving mothers and their children. There is no earthly love like a mother's love. It can only be compared to the love God has for His people (Isaiah 49:14-16). A mother's love is enduring.

E. GREEN 54-19

"NEXT TO GOD WE ARE INDEBTED TO WOMEN, FIRST FOR LIFE ITSELF, AND THEN FOR MAKING IT WORTH LIVING."   **Mary McLeod Bethune, Educator**

For this child I prayed; and the Lord hath given me my petition which I asked of him: Therefore also I have lent him to the Lord; as long as he liveth he shall be lent to the Lord. And he worshipped the Lord there.

1 Samuel 1:27-28

Her children arise up, and call her blessed; her husband also, and he praiseth her.

Proverbs 31:28

But Zion said, The Lord hath forsaken me, and my Lord hath forgotten me. Can a woman forget her sucking child, that she should not have compassion on the son of her womb? yea, they may forget, yet will I not forget thee. Behold, I have graven thee upon the palms of my hands; thy walls are continually before me.

Isaiah 49:14-16

But we were gentle among you, even as a nurse cherisheth her children.

1 Thessalonians 2:7

Promises from God for

Responsibility of Parenting

Parents should expose their children to positive role models. By role models, I do not mean entertainers or athletes. I mean parents, extended and augmented families, church leaders, and community members who have the opportunity to mold lives and change attitudes on a daily basis.... These are people who can exemplify and instill moral and spiritual values. These are people who can promote faith development and racial pride, by sharing their faith and ancestral stories. These are people who can demonstrate the importance of setting goals and reaching them. Certainly, these are people who can lend credence to the "It takes a village" concept. These are the role models that our young people need to see in action.

H. HARRIS 150-28

Excerpt from the *Women of Color Study Bible*

And thou shalt love the Lord thy God with all thine heart, and with all thy soul, and with all thy might. And these words, which I command thee this day, shall be in thine heart: And thou shalt teach them diligently unto thy children, and shalt talk of them when thou sittest in thine house, and when thou walkest by the way, and when thou liest down, and when thou risest up.

DEUTERONOMY 6:5-7

~

And said, Verily I say unto you, Except ye be converted, and become as little children, ye shall not enter into the kingdom of heaven.

MATTHEW 18:3

~

And, ye fathers, provoke not your children to wrath: but bring them up in the nurture and admonition of the Lord.

EPHESIANS 6:4

"SIMPLY HAVING CHILDREN DOES NOT NECESSARILY MAKE A WOMAN A MOTHER." **Mary Futrell, Educator**

Promises from God for

Teaching Children

God instructs us...to "lay hands" on our children—not the hands of violence that the enemy tries to "stress" us into, but hands guided by God's love to impart some spiritual gift. As we ask God to raise our children to glorify Him, mediate on the examples of Jesus, Lois, Eunice, and Paul. Teach children undying faith in the Father, provide them with godly associations, and lay hands on them and pray.

J. SCOTT 790-18

"CHILDREN COULD KEEP ON THE STRAIGHT AND NARROW PATH IF THEY COULD GET INFORMATION FROM SOMEONE WHO'S BEEN OVER THE ROUTE."

**Marian Wright Edelman,
Founder, Children's Defense Guild**

Excerpt from the *Women of Color Study Bible*

*By thee have I been holden up from the womb:
thou art he that took me out of my mother's
bowels: my praise shall be continually of thee.*

PSALM 71:6

~

*For he established a testimony in Jacob, and
appointed a law in Israel, which he commanded
our fathers, that they should make them known to
their children: That the generation to come might
know them, even the children which should be
born; who should arise and declare them to their
children: That they might set their hope in God,
and not forget the works of God, but keep
his commandments.*

PSALM 78:5-7

~

*For thou hast possessed my reins: thou hast cov-
ered me in my mother's womb.*

PSALM 139:13

~

*Verily I say unto you, Whosoever shall not receive
the kingdom of God as a little child, he
shall not enter therein.*

MARK 10:15

~

*Let no man despise thy youth; but be thou an
example of the believers, in word, in conversation,
in charity, in spirit, in faith, in purity.*

1 TIMOTHY 4:12

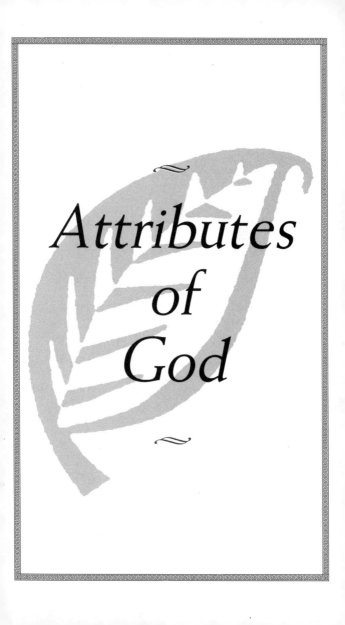

Attributes

of

God

Promises from God for

Authority

Through Jesus Christ, women have their framework for life. No matter how many pieces may seem to be mixed up, as long as we are guided by the smooth edges of God's Spirit, God's Word, and Christ's example, our hope is secure. God on the left, God on the right, God above, God beneath, God all around.

A. MIDDLETON 406-21

"IT'S PRETTY HARD FOR THE LORD TO GUIDE YOU IF YOU HAVEN'T MADE UP YOUR MIND WHICH WAY YOU WANT TO GO." **Madame C. J. Walker, Entrepreneur and Philanthropist**

Excerpt from the *Women of Color Study Bible*

He is the Rock, his work is perfect: for all his ways are judgment: a God of truth and without iniquity, just and right is he.

DEUTERONOMY 32:4

~

For the Lord God is a sun and shield: the Lord will give grace and glory: no good thing will he withhold from them that walk uprightly.

PSALM 84:11

~

The counsel of the Lord standeth for ever, the thoughts of his heart to all generations.

PSALM 33:11

~

For I know the thoughts that I think toward you, saith the Lord, thoughts of peace, and not of evil, to give you an expected end.

JEREMIAH 29:11

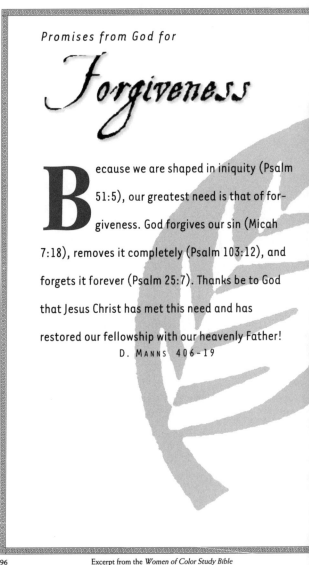

Promises from God for

Forgiveness

Because we are shaped in iniquity (Psalm 51:5), our greatest need is that of forgiveness. God forgives our sin (Micah 7:18), removes it completely (Psalm 103:12), and forgets it forever (Psalm 25:7). Thanks be to God that Jesus Christ has met this need and has restored our fellowship with our heavenly Father!

D. MANNS 406-19

Excerpt from the *Women of Color Study Bible*

*Purge me with hyssop, and I shall be clean: wash
me, and I shall be whiter than snow.*

PSALM 51:7

*I have blotted out, as a thick cloud, thy transgres-
sions, and, as a cloud, thy sins: return unto me;
for I have redeemed thee.*

ISAIAH 44:22

*Therefore also now, saith the Lord, turn ye even
to me with all your heart, and with fasting, and
with weeping, and with mourning: And rend your
heart, and not your garments, and turn unto the
Lord your God: for he is gracious and merciful,
slow to anger, and of great kindness, and   .
repenteth him of the evil.*

JOEL 2:12-13

*If we confess our sins, he is faithful and just to for-
give us our sins, and to cleanse us from all
unrighteousness.*

1 JOHN 1:9

Promises from God for

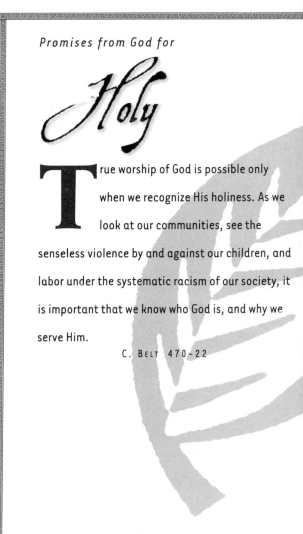

Holy

True worship of God is possible only when we recognize His holiness. As we look at our communities, see the senseless violence by and against our children, and labor under the systematic racism of our society, it is important that we know who God is, and why we serve Him.

C. BELT 470-22

Excerpt from the *Women of Color Study Bible*

Be still, and know that I am God: I will be exalted among the heathen, I will be exalted in the earth.

PSALM 46:10

~

Know ye that the Lord he is God: it is he that hath made us, and not we ourselves; we are his people, and the sheep of his pasture.

PSALM 100:3

~

To whom then will ye liken me, or shall I be equal? saith the Holy One.

ISAIAH 40:25

~

Am I a God at hand, saith the Lord, and not a God afar off? Can any hide himself in secret places that I shall not see him? saith the Lord. Do not I fill heaven and earth? saith the Lord.

JEREMIAH 23:23-24

~

*But as he which hath called you is holy, so be ye holy in all manner of conversation;
Because it is written, Be ye holy; for I am holy.*

1 PETER 1:15-16

Promises from God for

Justice

We have an expectation of what we consider "fair." Sometimes we are bewildered when God does not meet our expectations. God's authority does not operate within the confines of who we think He should be, because God is in control. God is accountable to no one and is supreme in authority, power, and rank (Psalm 115:3).

A. MIDDLETON 406-22

"GOD'S LAWS LAST LONGER THAN THOSE WHO BREAK THEM."

Charlotte E. Ray,
First African-American female lawyer

Excerpt from the *Women of Color Study Bible*

And God said unto Moses, I AM THAT I AM: and he said, Thus shalt thou say unto the children of Israel, I AM hath sent me unto you.

EXODUS 3:14

He is the Rock, his work is perfect: for all his ways are judgment: a God of truth and without iniquity, just and right is he.

DEUTERONOMY 32:4

For the righteous Lord loveth righteousness; his countenance doth behold the upright.

PSALM 11:7

And therefore will the Lord wait, that he may be gracious unto you, and therefore will he be exalted, that he may have mercy upon you: for the Lord is a God of judgment: blessed are all they that wait for him.

ISAIAH 30:18

Promises from God for

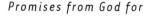

Love

God's love—bountiful, immeasurable, and unconditional—demonstrates how much He wants each one of His children to be saved. He made the supreme sacrifice of sending His only Son into a sinful world, not only to live an exemplary life but also to die that we might have eternal life. "Christ was treated as we deserve, that we might be treated as He deserves. He suffered the death which was ours that we might live the life which was His" (*The Desire of Ages*, p. 7). Such love, such grace!

R. ARMSTER 54-22

"THERE IS MORE PLEASURE IN LOVING THAN IN BEING LOVED." **Jeanne Moutoussamy-Ashe, Photographer and widow of former tennis great**

Thou wilt shew me the path of life: in thy presence is fulness of joy; at thy right hand there are pleasures for evermore.

PSALM 16:11

~

Behold, the eye of the Lord is upon them that fear him, upon them that hope in his mercy.

PSALM 33:18

~

The Lord is gracious, and full of compassion; slow to anger, and of great mercy.

PSALM 145:8

~

But God, who is rich in mercy, for his great love wherewith he loved us, Even when we were dead in sins, hath quickened us together with Christ, (by grace ye are saved).

EPHESIANS 2:4-5

~

Being confident of this very thing, that he which hath begun a good work in you will perform it until the day of Jesus Christ.

PHILIPPIANS 1:6

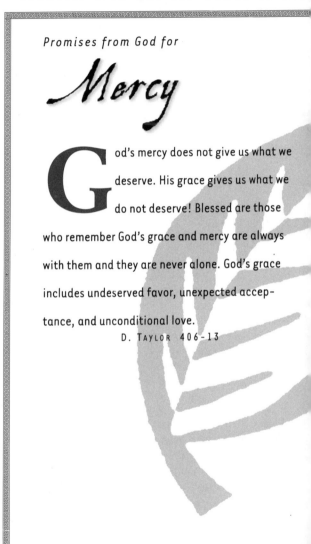

Promises from God for

Mercy

God's mercy does not give us what we deserve. His grace gives us what we do not deserve! Blessed are those who remember God's grace and mercy are always with them and they are never alone. God's grace includes undeserved favor, unexpected acceptance, and unconditional love.

D. TAYLOR 406-13

Surely goodness and mercy shall follow me all the days of my life: and I will dwell in the house of the Lord for ever.

PSALM 23:6

~

The Lord is gracious, and full of compassion; slow to anger, and of great mercy.

PSALM 145:8

~

Not by works of righteousness which we have done, but according to his mercy he saved us, by the washing of regeneration, and renewing of the Holy Ghost.

TITUS 3:5

~

Behold, we count them happy which endure. Ye have heard of the patience of Job, and have seen the end of the Lord; that the Lord is very pitiful, and of tender mercy.

JAMES 5:11

~

Blessed be the God and Father of our Lord Jesus Christ, which according to his abundant mercy hath begotten us again unto a lively hope by the resurrection of Jesus Christ from the dead.

1 PETER 1:3

Promises from God for

Omniscience

G od has perfect knowledge of all that transpires in human experiences. God does not have to reason, or find things out, or learn gradually. God's knowledge of past, present, and future is simultaneous. He learns from no one. He is never surprised and He never forgets (Isaiah 46:9-10). Every now and then, God chooses to share that knowledge with us.

B. WHIPPLE 790-20

"MY TOP PRIORITY IS TO ALIGN MYSELF WITH THE FATHER OF CREATION." **Jayne Kennedy Overton, Television Personality**

Excerpt from the *Women of Color Study Bible*

But the Lord said unto Samuel, Look not on his
countenance, or on the height of his stature;
because I have refused him: for the Lord seeth not
as man seeth; for man looketh on the outward
appearance, but the Lord looketh on the heart.

1 SAMUEL 16:7

The Lord is the portion of mine inheritance and of
my cup: thou maintainest my lot.

PSALM 16:5

The Lord looketh from heaven; he beholdeth all
the sons of men. From the place of his habitation
he looketh upon all the inhabitants of the earth.
He fashioneth their hearts alike; he considereth
all their works.

PSALM 33:13-15

Remember the former things of old: for I am God,
and there is none else; I am God, and there is
none like me, Declaring the end from the beginning, and from ancient times the things that are
not yet done, saying, My counsel shall stand,
and I will do all my pleasure.

ISAIAH 46:9-10

O the depth of the riches both of the wisdom and
knowledge of God! how unsearchable are his
judgments, and his ways past finding out!

ROMANS 11:33

Promises from God for

Patience

God desires that we reflect the image of the Holy Spirit that lives within us. The presence of the Holy Spirit should not be interpreted to mean that we wait with anxiety, irritation, confusion, or passive resignation. Waiting should not be understood as being done with jealousy, envy, or with rage. It is an active response to opposition. Waiting with the patience God grants is not without movement.

C. COOKE 406-20

But thou, O Lord, art a God full of compassion,
and gracious, longsuffering, and plenteous in
mercy and truth.

PSALM 86:15

~

I wait for the Lord, my soul doth wait, and in his
word do I hope. My soul waiteth for the Lord
more than they that watch for the morning: I say,
more than they that watch for the morning.

PSALM 130:5-6

~

Charity suffereth long, and is kind; charity envieth
not; charity vaunteth not itself, is not puffed up,
Doth not behave itself unseemly, seeketh not her
own, is not easily provoked, thinketh no evil;
Rejoiceth not in iniquity, but rejoiceth in the
truth; Beareth all things, believeth all things,
hopeth all things, endureth all things.

1 CORINTHIANS 13:4-7

~

Rejoicing in hope; patient in tribulation;
continuing instant in prayer.

ROMANS 12:12

~

Forbearing one another, and forgiving one
another, if any man have a quarrel against any:
even as Christ forgave you, so also do ye.

COLOSSIANS 3:13

Promises from God for

Presence

God is as close as the very air we breathe. We cannot experience a human emotion that God is outside of. In ways that are often incomprehensible at the time, God is present at the point of our greatest sense of brokenness and abandonment. The theology of the profound love of God understands that God has entered the drama and trauma of our lives and even screams with us in despair. Jesus, who was in the beginning with God, and who is indeed God, promises never to leave or forsake us. The profound love of God moved Him to take on flesh and hang on a cross where He screamed in agony, "My God, my God, why . . ." (Matthew 27:46).

C. SWAFFORD HARRIS 406-18

Yet the Lord will command his lovingkindness in the daytime, and in the night his song shall be with me, and my prayer unto the God of my life.

PSALM 42:8

～

For the mountains shall depart, and the hills be removed; but my kindness shall not depart from thee, neither shall the covenant of my peace be removed, saith the Lord that hath mercy on thee.

ISAIAH 54:10

～

Fear thou not; for I am with thee: be not dismayed; for I am thy God: I will strengthen thee; yea, I will help thee; yea, I will uphold thee with the right hand of my righteousness.

ISAIAH 41:10

～

When thou passest through the waters, I will be with thee; and through the rivers, they shall not overflow thee: when thou walkest through the fire, thou shalt not be burned; neither shall the flame kindle upon thee.

ISAIAH 43:2

"GOD SPEAKS WHEREVER HE FINDS A HUMBLE, LISTENING EAR. AND THE LANGUAGE HE USES IS KINDNESS."
Lena Horne, Singer

Promises from God for

Protection

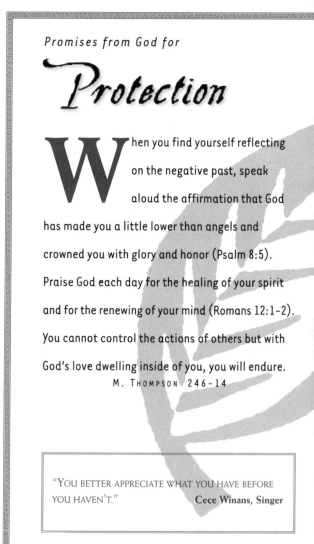

hen you find yourself reflecting on the negative past, speak aloud the affirmation that God has made you a little lower than angels and crowned you with glory and honor (Psalm 8:5). Praise God each day for the healing of your spirit and for the renewing of your mind (Romans 12:1-2). You cannot control the actions of others but with God's love dwelling inside of you, you will endure.

M. THOMPSON 246-14

"YOU BETTER APPRECIATE WHAT YOU HAVE BEFORE YOU HAVEN'T."   **Cece Winans, Singer**

Cast thy burden upon the Lord, and he shall
sustain thee: he shall never suffer the
righteous to be moved.

PSALM 55:22

Because he hath set his love upon me, therefore
will I deliver him: I will set him on high, because
he hath known my name. He shall call upon me,
and I will answer him: I will be with him in trouble;
I will deliver him, and honour him.

PSALM 91:14-15

And we know that all things work together for
good to them that love God, to them who are the
called according to his purpose.

ROMANS 8:28

Blessed be God, even the Father of our Lord Jesus
Christ, the Father of mercies, and the God of all
comfort; Who comforteth us in all our tribulation,
that we may be able to comfort them which are in
any trouble, by the comfort wherewith we
ourselves are comforted of God.

2 CORINTHIANS 1:3-4

Promises from God for

Provision

nticipate receiving the secret desires of your heart from the Lord. Take verses, like Psalm 37:4-5, to heart: "Delight thyself also in the Lord; and he shall give thee the desires of thine heart. Commit thy way unto the Lord; trust also in him; and he shall bring it to pass." Look for the needs in your life to be met. In fact, expect them. These blessings will come to you from your loving God who has your best interests at heart. "But my God shall supply all your needs according to his riches in glory by Christ Jesus," (Philippians 4:19).

S. ROBINSON 406-16

"EVERY DAY THAT DAWNS IS A REASON TO SAY, 'THANK YOU, FATHER.'" **Johnetta Cole, President, Spelman College**

Excerpt from the *Women of Color Study Bible*

*I sought the Lord, and he heard me, and
delivered me from all my fears.*

PSALM 34:4

~

*And the Lord shall guide thee continually, and
satisfy thy soul in drought, and make fat thy
bones: and thou shalt be like a watered garden,
and like a spring of water, whose waters fail not.*

ISAIAH 58:11

~

*Wherefore, if God so clothe the grass of the field,
which to day is, and to morrow is cast into the
oven, shall he not much more clothe you, O ye of
little faith? Therefore take no thought, saying,
What shall we eat? or, What shall we drink? or,
Wherewithal shall we be clothed? (For after all
these things do the Gentiles seek:) for your
heavenly Father knoweth that ye have need
of all these things.*

MATTHEW 6:30-32

~

*And God is able to make all grace abound toward
you; that ye, always having all sufficiency in all
things, may abound to every good work.*

2 CORINTHIANS 9:8

~

*But my God shall supply all your need according
to his riches in glory by Christ Jesus.*

PHILIPPIANS 4:19

Promises from God for

Righteousness

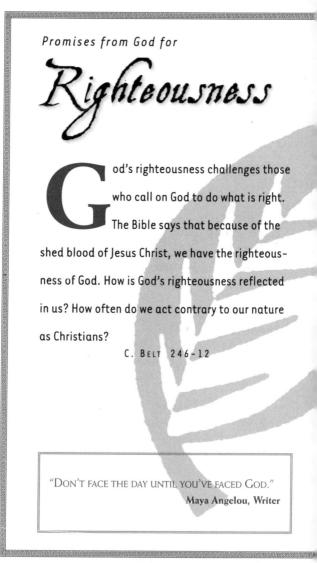

God's righteousness challenges those who call on God to do what is right. The Bible says that because of the shed blood of Jesus Christ, we have the righteousness of God. How is God's righteousness reflected in us? How often do we act contrary to our nature as Christians?

C. BELT 246-12

"DON'T FACE THE DAY UNTIL YOU'VE FACED GOD."

Maya Angelou, Writer

*For the righteous Lord loveth righteousness; his
countenance doth behold the upright.*
PSALM 11:7

∼

*Gracious is the Lord, and righteous; yea,
our God is merciful.*
PSALM 116:5

∼

*Even the righteousness of God which is by faith of
Jesus Christ unto all and upon all them that
believe: for there is no difference.*
ROMANS 3:22

∼

*But of him are ye in Christ Jesus, who of God is
made unto us wisdom, and righteousness, and
sanctification, and redemption.*
1 CORINTHIANS 1:30

∼

*For he hath made him to be sin for us, who knew
no sin; that we might be made the righteousness
of God in him.*
2 CORINTHIANS 5:21

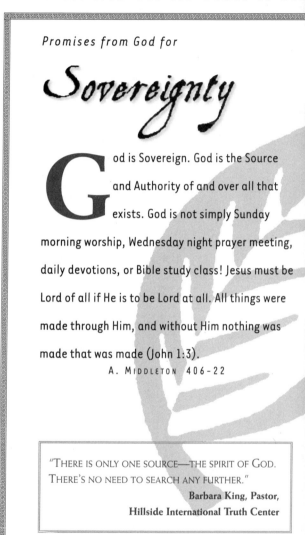

Promises from God for

Sovereignty

God is Sovereign. God is the Source and Authority of and over all that exists. God is not simply Sunday morning worship, Wednesday night prayer meeting, daily devotions, or Bible study class! Jesus must be Lord of all if He is to be Lord at all. All things were made through Him, and without Him nothing was made that was made (John 1:3).

A. MIDDLETON 406-22

"THERE IS ONLY ONE SOURCE—THE SPIRIT OF GOD. THERE'S NO NEED TO SEARCH ANY FURTHER."

**Barbara King, Pastor,
Hillside International Truth Center**

Which in his times he shall shew, who is the blessed and only Potentate, the King of kings, and Lord of lords; Who only hath immortality, dwelling in the light which no man can approach unto; whom no man hath seen, nor can see: to whom be honour and power everlasting. Amen.

1 TIMOTHY 6:15-16

For great is the Lord, and greatly to be praised: he also is to be feared above all gods.

1 CHRONICLES 16:25

Say unto God, How terrible art thou in thy works! through the greatness of thy power shall thine enemies submit themselves unto thee. All the earth shall worship thee, and shall sing unto thee; they shall sing to thy name.

PSALM 66:3-4

O come, let us worship and bow down: let us kneel before the Lord our maker. For he is our God; and we are the people of his pasture, and the sheep of his hand.

PSALM 95:6-7

Promises from God for

Truth

T

he Bible says, "The judgments of the LORD are true and righteous altogether. More to be desired are they than gold, yea, than much fine gold: sweeter also than honey and the honeycomb" (Psalm 19:9-10). These are words of assurance in a world where justice is for sale to the highest bidder, and righteousness is a scarce commodity. God's righteousness is immovable (Psalm 36:5-6). As the prophet Samuel pointed out to the people, God has always acted in a righteous manner when He has dealt with His people (see 1 Samuel 12:6-7). God's standards are nonnegotiable. His righteous nature assures us that God will always do what is right.

C. BELT 246-12

Excerpt from the *Women of Color Study Bible*

Righteous art thou, O Lord, and uprigh
are thy judgments.
PSALM 119:137

~

The Lord is righteous in all his ways, and holy
in all his works.
PSALM 145:17

~

Behold, the days come, saith the Lord, that I will
raise unto David a righteous Branch, and a King
shall reign and prosper, and shall execute
judgment and justice in the earth.
JEREMIAH 23:5

~

Not unto us, O Lord, not unto us, but unto thy
name give glory, for thy mercy, and for thy truth's
sake. Wherefore should the heathen say, Where is
now their God? But our God is in the heavens: he
hath done whatsoever he hath pleased.
PSALM 115:1-3

"IF NOW ISN'T A GOOD TIME FOR THE TRUTH, I
DON'T SEE WHEN WE'LL GET TO IT." **Nikki Giovanni,**
Poet, Lecturer, and Essayist

Relationship
Issues

Promises from God for

Aging

A woman's looks, health, and her circumstances change with time. Many women attempt to cope with these changes by clinging to outward beauty, youthful behaviors, and past achievements. However, once we realize that we are made in accordance with God's plan, and that plan carries us through the change of time, we come to grips with aging. Women, as well as others who live each day for the Lord, will not only bear fruit while they are young, they will also bear fruit in their old age (Psalm 92:12-15).

A. POWELL 470-20

Excerpt from the *Women of Color Study Bible*

*To every thing there is a season, and a time to
every purpose under the heaven.*

ECCLESSIASTES 3:1

❧

*The hoary head is a crown of glory, if it be found
in the way of righteousness.*

PROVERBS 16:31

❧

*Favour is deceitful, and beauty is vain: but a
woman that feareth the Lord, she shall be praised.*

PROVERBS 31:30

❧

*I will greatly rejoice in the Lord, my soul shall be
joyful in my God; for he hath clothed me with the
garments of salvation, he hath covered me with
the robe of righteousness, as a bridegroom
decketh himself with ornaments, and as a bride
adorneth herself with her jewels.*

ISAIAH 61:10

❧

*But let it be the hidden man of the heart, in that
which is not corruptible, even the ornament of a
meek and quiet spirit, which is in the sight
of God of great price.*

1 PETER 3:4

Promises from God for

Community

As believers in Christ, we know that God works through people on the opposite side of the political and economic power structure to create change and to move the world to new levels of civility. When we fervently pray and humble ourselves to God's will for our lives as Hannah did, we open ourselves to what God would have us give back to our communities. We give back to God by helping others and by becoming engaged in the struggle to create a political and economic system that recognizes the worth of all of God's children. By faithfully offering our best to God, like Hannah, we become empowered by God to create communities that reflect His love.

A. DAVIS 246-12

Excerpt from the *Women of Color Study Bible*

*But I say unto you, Love your enemies, bless them
that curse you, do good to them that hate you,
and pray for them which despitefully use you, and
persecute you; That ye may be the children of
your Father which is in heaven: for he maketh his
sun to rise on the evil and on the good, and
sendeth rain on the just and on the unjust.*

MATTHEW 5:44-45

*And as ye would that men should do to you,
do ye also to them likewise.*

LUKE 6:31

*Let us therefore follow after the things which
make for peace, and things wherewith
one may edify another.*

ROMANS 14:19

*If ye fulfil the royal law according to the scripture,
Thou shalt love thy neighbour as thyself,
ye do well.*

JAMES 2:8

"WE WILL BAND TOGETHER AND SURVIVE OR LIVE
APART AND DIE AS FOOLS." **Susan Taylor,**
Editor-in-Chief, Essence Magazine

Promises from God for

Elderly

The footprints of other faithful pilgrims illuminate, inform, and enrich our lives, leaving a legacy of commitment to those things that are "true, whatsoever things are honest, whatsoever things are just, whatsoever things are pure" (Philippians 4:8). We are, therefore, challenged to do likewise. As we age, let us do so with grace, striving to use our gift of time to honor God and uplift others. Then one day our lives will be counted and remembered as testimonies of love and service, as we make our footprints on the sands of time.

A. POWELL 470-20

Excerpt from the *Women of Color Study Bible*

*O God, thou hast taught me from my youth: and
hitherto have I declared thy wondrous works.
Now also when I am old and greyheaded, O God,
forsake me not; until I have shewed thy strength
unto this generation, and thy power to every
one that is to come.*

PSALM 71:17-18

*The righteous shall flourish like the palm tree: he
shall grow like a cedar in Lebanon. Those that be
planted in the house of the Lord shall flourish in
the courts of our God. They shall still bring forth
fruit in old age; they shall be fat and flourishing;
To shew that the Lord is upright: he is my rock,
and there is no unrighteousness in him.*

PSALM 92:12-15

*Wherefore I perceive that there is nothing better,
than that a man should rejoice in his own works;
for that is his portion: for who shall bring him to
see what shall be after him?*

ECCLESIASTES 3:22

*And even to your old age I am he; and even to
hoar hairs will I carry you: I have made, and I will
bear; even I will carry, and will deliver you.*

ISAIAH 46:4

Promises from God for

Friendship

Ruth and Naomi were friends that loved at all times—in good and bad situations. Their actions freely demonstrated the self-sacrificing love that builds intimacy in any relationship. This type of love would "lay down his life for his friend" as Jesus spoke of (see John 15:13). Intimacy bears with it the great possibility for great pain. Betrayal is so much more hurtful when it comes at the hand of a trusted, intimate friend (Psalm 55:12-14). Intimate friendship is disrupted by petty disputation, lack of trustworthiness (Proverbs 11:13), withholding kindness (Job 6:14), and whispering or gossip (Proverbs 16:28). All of these things are intimacy breakers.

E. ALEXANDER 150-30

Greater love hath no man than this, that a man lay down his life for his friends.

JOHN 15:13

∼

He loveth transgression that loveth strife: and he that exalteth his gate seeketh destruction.

PROVERBS 17:19

∼

Iron sharpeneth iron; so a man sharpeneth the countenance of his friend.

PROVERBS 27:17

∼

For where two or three are gathered together in my name, there am I in the midst of them.

MATTHEW 18:20

∼

If I then, your Lord and Master, have washed your feet; ye also ought to wash one another's feet. For I have given you an example, that ye should do as I have done to you.

JOHN 13:14-15

"NO PERSON IS YOUR FRIEND WHO DEMANDS YOUR SILENCE, OR DENIES YOUR RIGHT TO GROW."

Alice Walker, Pulitzer Prize-winning Author and Activist

Promises from God for

Love for Others

When we express our love to others, we allow God's love to shine through us (1 John 3:14; 4:7, 20). All through the Bible we are shown God's love and told to show His love to others: our friends and family—even those who may not like us or whom we dislike. The Bible not only tells us to love, it tells us how to love (1 John 3:18; 4:7-8). This day, why not sing out loud, or just in your mind, the little song: " 'Tis Love That Makes Us Happy." The words are:

God is love; we're His little children.

God is love; we would be like Him.

'Tis love that makes us happy,

'Tis love that smoothes the way;

It helps us mind, it makes us kind

To others every day. —F. E. BELDEN, 1892
E. WATSON 854-31

*Let nothing be done through strife or vainglory;
but in lowliness of mind let each esteem other
better than themselves. Look not every man on
his own things, but every man also on the
things of others.*

PHILIPPIANS 2:3-4

~

*No man hath seen God at any time. If we
love one another, God dwelleth in us, and his
love is perfected in us.*

1 JOHN 4:12

~

*Hereby perceive we the love of God, because he
laid down his life for us: and we ought to lay down
our lives for the brethren. But whoso hath this
world's good, and seeth his brother have need,
and shutteth up his bowels of compassion from
him, how dwelleth the love of God in him?
My little children, let us not love in word,
neither in tongue; but in deed and in truth.*

1 JOHN 3:16-18

"SOME OF US AREN'T PREPARED TO ACCEPT SUCCESS
—ESPECIALLY SOMEONE ELSE'S."

Sarah Vaughan, Jazz Legend

Promises from God for

Restoration

We, the women of the African American community, must also take a holistic approach to restoring our communities. Restoring the institutions, our walls, is necessary to make our communities economically viable and financially stable. But restoring the institutions is not the only issue. Until the people have restored their relationship with God, the rebuilding process is incomplete—a patchwork solution at best.

D. JOHNSON   374-8

"HONEY, IT'S SO EASY TO TALK A GOOD GAME. WHAT WE NEED ARE FOLKS WHO WILL DO SOMETHING!"
Maxine Waters, Congresswoman

Excerpt from the *Women of Color Study Bible*

Pray for the peace of Jerusalem: they shall prosper that love thee. Peace be within thy walls, and prosperity within thy palaces. For my brethren and companions' sakes, I will now say, Peace be within thee. Because of the house of the Lord our God I will seek thy good.

PSALM 122:6-9

~

Behold, how good and how pleasant it is for brethren to dwell together in unity!

PSALM 133:1

~

That their hearts might be comforted, being knit together in love, and unto all riches of the full assurance of understanding, to the acknowledgement of the mystery of God, and of the Father, and of Christ.

COLOSSIANS 2:2

~

As every man hath received the gift, even so minister the same one to another, as good stewards of the manifold grace of God.

1 PETER 4:10

Promises from God for

Sisterhood

omen need the fellowship—the nurturing companionship of other women. Above all things we need the fellowship of God (see Leviticus 26:11-13; 1 John 1:3). Friendship between two women is based on love, loyalty, and commitment. An example of a devoted friendship between two women is seen in the New Testament between Elisabeth and Mary (Luke 1:39-56), and in the Old Testament between Ruth and Naomi, a mother-in law/daughter-in-law situation that blossomed into a lifelong friendship. African-American Christian women are encouraged to build lasting friendships that will endure life's challenges.

A. HOWELL 406-11

*A friend loveth at all times, and a brother
is born for adversity.*
PROVERBS 17:17

~

*A man that hath friends must shew himself
friendly: and there is a friend that sticketh
closer than a brother.*
PROVERBS 18:24

~

*Two are better than one; because they have a
good reward for their labour. For if they fall, the
one will lift up his fellow: but woe to him that is
alone when he falleth; for he hath not another
to help him up.*
ECCLESIASTES 4:9-10

~

*Let nothing be done through strife or vainglory;
but in lowliness of mind let each esteem other
better than themselves. Look not every man on
his own things, but every man also on the
things of others.*
PHILIPPIANS 2:3-4

"WE CANNOT SILENCE THE VOICES THAT WE DO NOT
LIKE HEARING. WE CAN, HOWEVER, DO EVERYTHING
IN OUR POWER TO MAKE CERTAIN OTHER VOICES ARE
HEARD." **Deborah Prophrow-Stith M.D., Dean of
Harvard School of Public Health**

Promises from God for

Unity of Believers

While we cannot be intimate with a host of people, there is a level of intimacy or communion that Christians can enjoy with each other based on our common heritage and faith. This kind of intimate love is not superficial—it comes from the heart (1 Peter 1:22). Jesus desired that all members of the church share in this kind of closeness that would allow the world to see a different way of being in relationship. His prayer was that we would be one, knitted together in love, as He and the Father are one (John 10:30).

E. ALEXANDER 822-25

Finally, brethren, farewell. Be perfect, be of good comfort, be of one mind, live in peace; and the God of love and peace shall be with you.

2 CORINTHIANS 13:11

~

There is neither Jew nor Greek, there is neither bond nor free, there is neither male nor female: for ye are all one in Christ Jesus.

GALATIANS 3:28

~

There is one body, and one Spirit, even as ye are called in one hope of your calling; One Lord, one faith, one baptism, One God and Father of all, who is above all, and through all, and in you all.

EPHESIANS 4:4-6

~

Seeing ye have purified your souls in obeying the truth through the Spirit unto unfeigned love of the brethren, see that ye love one another with a pure heart fervently.

1 PETER 1:22

*What the
Bible
Says
About...*

Promises from God for

Anger

When confronted by circumstances or situations that you perceive as unjust, don't react too quickly even though you may feel hurt or threatened. Don't follow your first impulse to curse. This angry response is sinful. Wait on the Lord. Anger may boil within, but praise the Lord. We need to ask ourselves if we are willing to trust God enough to release our anger into His care. Can we focus on the energy our anger produces into positive action? We need to be constant in prayer so that, when we are bumped, what spills out is wisdom from on high. "The mouth of the just bringeth forth wisdom" (Proverbs 10:31).

J. WOOD 54-23

The preparations of the heart in man, and the answer of the tongue, is from the Lord. All the ways of a man are clean in his own eyes; but the Lord weigheth the spirits. Commit thy works unto the Lord, and thy thoughts shall be established.

PROVERBS 16:1-3

And they that are Christ's have crucified the flesh with the affections and lusts. If we live in the Spirit, let us also walk in the Spirit. Let us not be desirous of vain glory, provoking one another, envying one another.

GALATIANS 5:24-26

And grieve not the holy Spirit of God, whereby ye are sealed unto the day of redemption. Let all bitterness, and wrath, and anger, and clamour, and evil speaking, be put away from you, with all malice: And be ye kind one to another, tenderhearted, forgiving one another, even as God for Christ's sake hath forgiven you.

EPHESIANS 4:30-32

Wherefore, my beloved brethren, let every man be swift to hear, slow to speak, slow to wrath.

JAMES 1:19

Promises from God for

Beauty

For women of color, reclaiming the power of self-image is one of the first steps to discovering a loving relationship with God. Self-image is intricately connected to standards of beauty; and for African women the world over, images and definitions of beauty are used to separate us from the love of God and ourselves.

I. CARRUTHERS 822-29

"CEASE TO BE A DRUDGE, SEEK TO BE AN ARTIST."

Mary McLeod Bethune, Educator

Excerpt from the *Women of Color Study Bible*

And God said, Let us make man in our image,
after our likeness: and let them have dominion
over the fish of the sea, and over the fowl of the
air, and over the cattle, and over all the earth,
and over every creeping thing that creepeth
upon the earth.

GENESIS 1:26

~

But the Lord said unto Samuel, Look not on his
countenance, or on the height of his stature;
because I have refused him: for the Lord seeth not
as man seeth; for man looketh on the outward
appearance, but the Lord looketh on the heart.

1 SAMUEL 16:7

~

Favour is deceitful, and beauty is vain: but a
woman that feareth the Lord, she shall be praised.

PROVERBS 31:30

~

Put on therefore, as the elect of God, holy and
beloved, bowels of mercies, kindness, humbleness
of mind, meekness, longsuffering.

COLOSSIANS 3:12

Promises from God for

Busyness

Alleviating stress begins with learning to say "no" and recognizing your strengths and limitations. By taking time out to revive ourselves—spiritually, mentally, emotionally, and physically—we are actually doing our loved ones a favor because we are better equipped to attend to their needs. When we are tired, it is harder for our light to shine before others as the Bible commands us (see Matthew 5:16).

J. ANDERSON-BLAIR 470-24

"THE ONLY WAY TO CATCH A COLD IS TO CHASE ONE." **Helen Carry, Minister, Christ Universal Temple**

Excerpt from the *Women of Color Study Bible*

I will both lay me down in peace, and sleep: for thou, Lord, only makest me dwell in safety.

PSALM 4:8

He that followeth after righteousness and mercy findeth life, righteousness, and honour.

PROVERBS 21:21

No man can serve two masters: for either he will hate the one, and love the other; or else he will hold to the one, and despise the other. Ye cannot serve God and mammon.

MATTHEW 6:24

These things I have spoken unto you, that in me ye might have peace. In the world ye shall have tribulation: but be of good cheer; I have overcome the world.

JOHN 16:33

And let the peace of God rule in your hearts, to the which also ye are called in one body; and be ye thankful.

COLOSSIANS 3:15

Promises from God for

Confidence

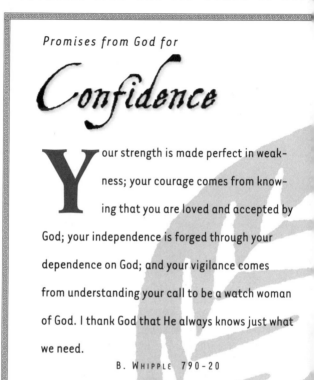

Your strength is made perfect in weakness; your courage comes from knowing that you are loved and accepted by God; your independence is forged through your dependence on God; and your vigilance comes from understanding your call to be a watch woman of God. I thank God that He always knows just what we need.

B. WHIPPLE 790-20

> "WE MUST CONQUER OUR OWN DOUBTS AND FEARS. IT IS THE GREATEST MISTAKE TO SIT AND DO NOTHING. EACH OF US MUST DO WHAT WE CAN."
>
> **Jane Browning Smith, Director, Inroads, Inc.**

Excerpt from the *Women of Color Study Bible*

O the depth of the riches both of the wisdom and knowledge of God! how unsearchable are his judgments, and his ways past finding out!

ROMANS 11:33

❦

It is God that girdeth me with strength, and maketh my way perfect. He maketh my feet like hinds' feet, and setteth me upon my high places.

PSALM 18:32-33

❦

The Lord is my light and my salvation; whom shall I fear? the Lord is the strength of my life; of whom shall I be afraid?

PSALM 27:1

❦

For the arms of the wicked shall be broken: but the Lord upholdeth the righteous. The Lord knoweth the days of the upright: and their inheritance shall be for ever. They shall not be ashamed in the evil time: and in the days of famine they shall be satisfied.

PSALM 37:17-19

❦

There is no fear in love; but perfect love casteth out fear: because fear hath torment. He that feareth is not made perfect in love. We love him, because he first loved us.

1 JOHN 4:18-19

Promises from God for

Giving

How blessed we are when we realize that everything we have belongs to God and has been loaned to us to share with others. When we arrive at this point, we are able to discern and to apply the liberating principle: be in bondage to no one—individually and collectively. For Christ has set us free. Let us therefore handle money in our private and corporate lives in a manner that reflects the liberty that is found in our relationship with Jesus Christ. Giving to others without a judging attitude will bring a woman abundant joy!

A. SIMS 598-24

He that giveth unto the poor shall not lack: but he
that hideth his eyes shall have many a curse.

PROVERBS 28:27

~

Give to every man that asketh of thee; and of him
that taketh away thy goods ask them not again.

LUKE 6:30

~

Give, and it shall be given unto you; good measure, pressed down, and shaken together, and run-
ning over, shall men give into your bosom. For
with the same measure that ye mete withal it shall
be measured to you again.

LUKE 6:38

~

But this I say, He which soweth sparingly shall
reap also sparingly; and he which soweth bountifully shall reap also bountifully. Every man according as he purposeth in his heart, so let him give;
not grudgingly, or of necessity: for God
loveth a cheerful giver.

2 CORINTHIANS 9:6-7

"WE MAKE A LIVING BY WHAT WE GET, BUT WE MAKE
A LIFE BY WHAT WE GIVE." **Barbara Harris, First
African-American Female Protestant Episcopal Bishop**

Promises from God for

Guidance

I have grown weary of bumping into the omnipotence of God and finding that God really does know best, that His ways are not my ways, and His thoughts are not my thoughts. I now live a surrendered life to God's will. There is nothing that I will encounter that God is not Lord over.

K. HAYES 406-20

IT'S BETTER TO BE PREPARED FOR AN OPPORTUNITY AND NOT HAVE ONE, THAN TO HAVE AN OPPORTUNITY AND NOT BE PREPARED." **Whitney Young, Founder, National Urban League**

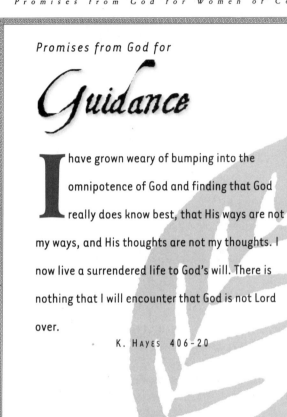

Excerpt from the *Women of Color Study Bible*

*Among the gods there is none like unto thee, O
Lord; neither are there any works like unto thy
works. All nations whom thou hast made shall
come and worship before thee, O Lord; and shall
glorify thy name. For thou art great, and doest
wondrous things: thou art God alone.*

PSALM 86:8-10

*Know ye that the Lord he is God: it is he that
hath made us, and not we ourselves; we are his
people, and the sheep of his pasture.*

PSALM 100:3

*For I know the thoughts that I think toward you,
saith the Lord, thoughts of peace, and not of evil,
to give you an expected end.*

JEREMIAH 29:11

*If I take the wings of the morning, and dwell in the
uttermost parts of the sea; Even there shall thy
hand lead me, and thy right hand shall hold me.*

PSALM 139:9-10

*Let no man say when he is tempted, I am tempted
of God: for God cannot be tempted with evil,
neither tempteth he any man.*

JAMES 1:13

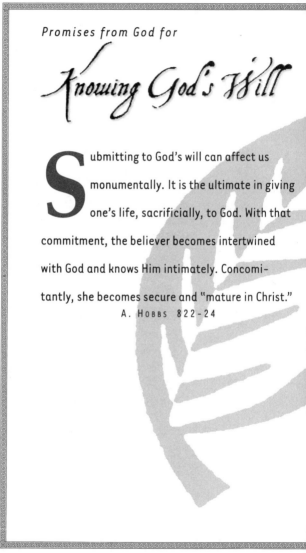

Promises from God for

Knowing God's Will

Submitting to God's will can affect us monumentally. It is the ultimate in giving one's life, sacrificially, to God. With that commitment, the believer becomes intertwined with God and knows Him intimately. Concomitantly, she becomes secure and "mature in Christ."

A. HOBBS 822-24

And this is the will of him that sent me, that every
one which seeth the Son, and believeth on him,
may have everlasting life: and I will raise him up
at the last day.

JOHN 6:40

~

And be not conformed to this world: but be ye
transformed by the renewing of your mind, that ye
may prove what is that good, and acceptable,
and perfect, will of God.

ROMANS 12:2

~

And they that are Christ's have crucified the flesh
with the affections and lusts.

GALATIANS 5:24

~

That we henceforth be no more children, tossed
to and fro, and carried about with every wind of
doctrine, by the sleight of men, and cunning
craftiness, whereby they lie in wait to deceive;
But speaking the truth in love, may grow up into
him in all things, which is the head, even Christ.

EPHESIANS 4:14-16

Promises from God for

Leadership

Women of color face special challenges in the journey through life. Learning the important principles of responsible decision making, delegation, and teamwork requires prayerful deliberation, strategic thinking, and dialogue with trusted mentors and friends. God has given us the gift of discernment in our decision making, creative thinking for our choices, and the ability to seek out allies and colleagues who will work with us in the professional arena.

M. NEWBERN-WILLIAMS 278-16

> "OF ALL THE QUALITIES NECESSARY FOR SUCCESS, NONE COMES BEFORE CHARACTER." **Ernesta Procope, CEO, E. G. Bowman Company**

Excerpt from the *Women of Color Study Bible*

*And if it seem evil unto you to serve the Lord,
choose you this day whom ye will serve; whether
the gods which your fathers served that were on
the other side of the flood, or the gods of the
Amorites, in whose land ye dwell: but as for me
and my house, we will serve the Lord.*

JOSHUA 24:15

*Ye have not chosen me, but I have chosen you,
and ordained you, that ye should go and bring
forth fruit, and that your fruit should remain: that
whatsoever ye shall ask of the Father in my
name, he may give it you.*

JOHN 15:16

*The integrity of the upright shall guide them:
but the perverseness of transgressors
shall destroy them.*

PROVERBS 11:3

*These are the things that ye shall do; Speak ye
every man the truth to his neighbour; execute the
judgment of truth and peace in your gates.*

ZECHARIAH 8:16

*With good will doing service, as to the Lord,
and not to men.*

EPHESIANS 6:7

Promises from God for

National Heritage

The very survival of our race compels us as parents and "village communities" to accept the challenge to help our youth understand that African-Americans in the past suffered, bled, and died in order for us to enter the door to opportunity today via education. Because of this, they do not have the right to nullify sacrifices made on our behalf by previous generations of African-Americans. Moreover, we must fulfill the mandates reflected in Deuteronomy 6:5-6 and Psalm 78:1-4. These mandates, coupled with our empowerment efforts, will not only sustain our heritage, but they will also be one of the greatest legacies that we can bequeath.

H. HARRIS 150-28

Excerpt from the *Women of Color Study Bible*

And that thou mayest tell in the ears of thy son,
and of thy son's son, what things I have wrought
in Egypt, and my signs which I have done among
them; that ye may know how that I am the Lord.

EXODUS 10:2

~

One generation shall praise thy works to another,
and shall declare thy mighty acts.

PSALM 145:4

~

The just man walketh in his integrity: his children
are blessed after him.

PROVERBS 20:7

~

Train up a child in the way he should go: and
when he is old, he will not depart from it.

PROVERBS 22:6

~

We will not hide them from their children, shew-
ing to the generation to come the praises of the
Lord, and his strength, and his wonderful
works that he hath done.

PSALM 78:4

"THIS COLORED PEOPLE GOING TO BE A PEOPLE."
Sojourner Truth, Abolitionist and Preacher

Promises from God for

Security

Instead of looking for security in tangible things that are only temporary, God wants us to know, love, and lean on Him, not just as Father and Savior but as soul mate, first love, best friend, and comforter (see Isaiah 54:1-6; John 14:26). He may use marriage to picture for us the eternal relationship between ourselves and our Savior, or He may call us to a single-minded, wholehearted focus on Him through celibacy (1 Corinthians 7:32-34). God points us through both callings to a final eternal union with Him, which He is preparing for us all.

C. RICHARDS 822-23

*For thy Maker is thine husband; the Lord of hosts
is his name; and thy Redeemer the Holy One
of Israel; The God of the whole earth
shall he be called.*

ISAIAH 54:5

*I will greatly rejoice in the Lord, my soul shall be
joyful in my God; for he hath clothed me with the
garments of salvation, he hath covered me with
the robe of righteousness, as a bridegroom
decketh himself with ornaments, and as a bride
adorneth herself with her jewels.*

ISAIAH 61:10

*And I will betroth thee unto me for ever; yea, I
will betroth thee unto me in righteousness, and in
judgment, and in lovingkindness, and in mercies.
I will even betroth thee unto me in faithfulness:
and thou shalt know the Lord.*

HOSEA 2:19-20

*Teaching them to observe all things whatsoever I
have commanded you: and, lo, I am with you
alway, even unto the end of the world. Amen.*

MATTHEW 28:20

Promises from God for

Self Worth

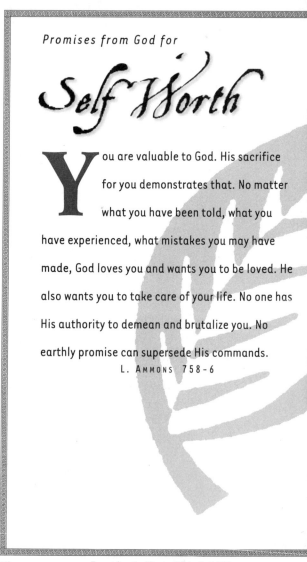

You are valuable to God. His sacrifice for you demonstrates that. No matter what you have been told, what you have experienced, what mistakes you may have made, God loves you and wants you to be loved. He also wants you to take care of your life. No one has His authority to demean and brutalize you. No earthly promise can supersede His commands.

L. AMMONS 758-6

So God created man in his own image, in the image of God created he him; male and female created he them.
GENESIS 1:27

~

For thou art an holy people unto the Lord thy God, and the Lord hath chosen thee to be a peculiar people unto himself, above all the nations that are upon the earth.
DEUTERONOMY 14:2

~

Before I formed thee in the belly I knew thee; and before thou camest forth out of the womb I sanctified thee, and I ordained thee a prophet unto the nations.
JEREMIAH 1:5

~

Wherefore thou art no more a servant, but a son; and if a son, then an heir of God through Christ.
GALATIANS 4:7

~

For God so loved the world, that he gave his only begotten Son, that whosoever believeth in him should not perish, but have everlasting life.
JOHN 3:16

Promises from God for

Single Life

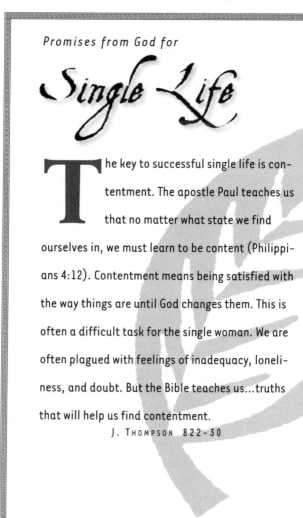

The key to successful single life is contentment. The apostle Paul teaches us that no matter what state we find ourselves in, we must learn to be content (Philippians 4:12). Contentment means being satisfied with the way things are until God changes them. This is often a difficult task for the single woman. We are often plagued with feelings of inadequacy, loneliness, and doubt. But the Bible teaches us...truths that will help us find contentment.

J. THOMPSON 822-30

*But ye are a chosen generation, a royal priesthood,
an holy nation, a peculiar people; that ye should
shew forth the praises of him who hath called you
out of darkness into his marvellous light.*

1 PETER 2:9

*And the Lord God said, It is not good that the
man should be alone; I will make him an
help meet for him.*

GENESIS 2:18

*Delight thyself also in the Lord; and he shall give
thee the desires of thine heart. Commit thy way
unto the Lord; trust also in him; and he shall bring
it to pass. And he shall bring forth thy righteousness as the light, and thy judgment as the noonday.*

PSALM 37:4-6

*But seek ye first the kingdom of God, and his
righteousness; and all these things shall be
added unto you.*

MATTHEW 6:33

*Be careful for nothing; but in every thing by
prayer and supplication with thanksgiving let your
requests be made known unto God.*

PHILIPPIANS 4:6

Promises from God for

Singleness

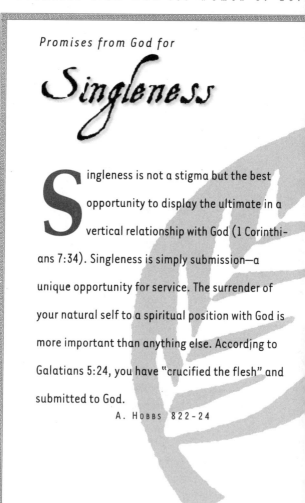

S ingleness is not a stigma but the best opportunity to display the ultimate in a vertical relationship with God (1 Corinthians 7:34). Singleness is simply submission—a unique opportunity for service. The surrender of your natural self to a spiritual position with God is more important than anything else. According to Galatians 5:24, you have "crucified the flesh" and submitted to God.

A. HOBBS 822-24

Excerpt from the *Women of Color Study Bible*

What? know ye not that your body is the temple of the Holy Ghost which is in you, which ye have of God, and ye are not your own? For ye are bought with a price: therefore glorify God in your body, and in your spirit, which are God's.

1 CORINTHIANS 6:19-20

~

There is difference also between a wife and a virgin. The unmarried woman careth for the things of the Lord, that she may be holy both in body and in spirit: but she that is married careth for the things of the world, how she may please her husband.

1 CORINTHIANS 7:34

~

Nevertheless I am continually with thee: thou hast holden me by my right hand.

PSALM 73:23

~

But I would have you without carefulness. He that is unmarried careth for the things that belong to the Lord, how he may please the Lord.

1 CORINTHIANS 7:32

~

As every man hath received the gift, even so minister the same one to another, as good stewards of the manifold grace of God.

1 PETER 4:10

Promises from God for

Suffering

How does one remain patient in view of continuous, seemingly endless, suffering? Asking one to be patient in the midst of suffering is a difficult request. Remember that even in suffering, the sovereignty of God prevails. Job persevered and was finally able to see what the Lord had in His divine plan for him. We may not understand the reasons why, but rest assured that God is full of mercy and compassion. God is your help in every need. (See Psalm 46:10.) God feeds your every hunger. God walks beside you night and day through every moment of your way. Even in our suffering, God is with us.

A. GORDON 406-11

Be still, and know that I am God: I will be exalted among the heathen, I will be exalted in the earth.

PSALM 46:10

I am the good shepherd: the good shepherd giveth his life for the sheep.

JOHN 10:11

For the mountains shall depart, and the hills be removed; but my kindness shall not depart from thee, neither shall the covenant of my peace be removed, saith the Lord that hath mercy on thee.

ISAIAH 54:10

It is of the Lord's mercies that we are not consumed, because his compassions fail not. They are new every morning: great is thy faithfulness.

LAMENTATIONS 3:22-23

Blessed are they that mourn: for they shall be comforted. Blessed are the meek: for they shall inherit the earth. Blessed are they which do hunger and thirst after righteousness: for they shall be filled.

MATTHEW 5:4-6

"DON'T BE UPSET IF YOUR DREAMS DON'T COME TRUE. IT COULD BE THE BEST THING THAT EVER HAPPENED TO YOU." **Shari Belafonte, Actress**

Promises from God for

Thoughts

If you think you can, you will. But if you think you can't, you won't. Christian women should be positive thinkers (Philippians 4:11-13). We should keep our minds on things that are true, noble, just, pure, lovely, and of good report (Philippians 4:8). Negative thinking will always keep you from overcoming the obstacles in your life, achieving your highest potential, and being free. The key to rising above your circumstances is to be renewed in your mind....Change your way of thinking from the negative to the positive (Philippians 4:8), and finally live each day by faith in God with whom nothing is impossible. Nothing will be impossible to the person who believes (Matthew 17:20; Mark 10:27).

C. BELT 790-21

Excerpt from the *Women of Color Study Bible*

And be not conformed to this world: but be ye
transformed by the renewing of your mind, that ye
may prove what is that good, and acceptable,
and perfect, will of God.

ROMANS 12:2

I can do all things through Christ which
strengtheneth me.

PHILIPPIANS 4:13

For as he thinketh in his heart, so is he: Eat and
drink, saith he to thee; but his heart is
not with thee.

PROVERBS 23:7

For to be carnally minded is death; but to be
spiritually minded is life and peace.

ROMANS 8:6

Casting down imaginations, and every high thing
that exalteth itself against the knowledge of God,
and bringing into captivity every thought to
the obedience of Christ.

2 CORINTHIANS 10:5

"WE USUALLY SEE THINGS NOT AS THEY ARE BUT AS
WE ARE." **Louise Beavers, Silent-Film Star**

Promises from God for

Truth

Though the gift of pleasing and flowing words might be from God, sometimes these words guide us in the wrong direction—away from God. God is, and will always be, the Creator. Although the First Mover is intrinsically involved in the "new," not every novel idea is from God. Examine the message of anyone you might think to follow. Are they speaking basic truths? Will following their lead be beneficial for all concerned? Above all, are they sent by Christ to help you on this journey back to Him and wholeness?

A. ADAMS-MORRIS 150-28

> "TRUTH-TELLERS ARE NOT ALWAYS PALATABLE. THERE IS A PREFERENCE FOR CANDY BARS."
>
> **Gwendolyn Brooks, Poet and Writer**

Buy the truth, and sell it not; also wisdom, and instruction, and understanding.

PROVERBS 23:23

And ye shall know the truth, and the truth shall make you free.

JOHN 8:32

Jesus saith unto him, I am the way, the truth, and the life: no man cometh unto the Father, but by me.

JOHN 14:6

Howbeit when he, the Spirit of truth, is come, he will guide you into all truth: for he shall not speak of himself; but whatsoever he shall hear, that shall he speak: and he will shew you things to come.

JOHN 16:13

And we know that the Son of God is come, and hath given us an understanding, that we may know him that is true, and we are in him that is true, even in his Son Jesus Christ. This is the true God, and eternal life.

1 JOHN 5:20

Promises from God for

Vanity

anity is a product of our will. As women, we must choose whether the center of our affections will be self or God. In our vanity, we misunderstand the gifts that God has given to us. We make them into idols and worship them. They, in turn, serve to separate us from ourselves, each other, and from God. We are gifted—not by the mere appearance of our faces and bodies—but by the love of God who created us, the forgiveness of Christ Jesus who liberates us, and the presence of the Holy Spirit who sustains us.

D. TAYLOR 726-8

"IT'S WHEN WE FORGET OURSELVES THAT WE ACCOMPLISH TASKS THAT ARE MOST LIKELY TO BE REMEMBERED."

Bessie Coleman,
First African-American Female Aviator

Excerpt from the *Women of Color Study Bible*

But the Lord said unto Samuel, Look not on his countenance, or on the height of his stature; because I have refused him: for the Lord seeth not as man seeth; for man looketh on the outward appearance, but the Lord looketh on the heart.

1 SAMUEL 16:7

Favour is deceitful, and beauty is vain: but a woman that feareth the Lord, she shall be praised.

PROVERBS 31:30

But we all, with open face beholding as in a glass the glory of the Lord, are changed into the same image from glory to glory, even as by the Spirit of the Lord.

2 CORINTHIANS 3:18

For we are his workmanship, created in Christ Jesus unto good works, which God hath before ordained that we should walk in them.

EPHESIANS 2:10

But let it be the hidden man of the heart, in that which is not corruptible, even the ornament of a meek and quiet spirit, which is in the sight of God of great price.

1 PETER 3:4

Promises from God for

Words We Say

How can we obtain such great salvation? By a part of our bodies that so easily besets and ensnares us. It is also the part of our bodies that can help us to leave the power of darkness and bring us into the marvelous light: by our mouths....It's a simple truth, but when we were saved, we had to say it—confess that Jesus, the Son of God, died and was raised from the dead three days later. We did not get saved just by thinking that we were saved; we confessed our salvation....Being a silent Christian, just like silently being saved, is impossible. We must confess—if not now, very soon. For saved or unsaved, every knee will bow and every tongue shall confess that Jesus is Lord.

C. BYRD 790-19

That if thou shalt confess with thy mouth the Lord Jesus, and shalt believe in thine heart that God hath raised him from the dead, thou shalt be saved. For with the heart man believeth unto righteousness; and with the mouth confession is made unto salvation.

ROMANS 10:9-10

~

Let no corrupt communication proceed out of your mouth, but that which is good to the use of edifying, that it may minister grace unto the hearers.

EPHESIANS 4:29

~

If any man speak, let him speak as the oracles of God; if any man minister, let him do it as of the ability which God giveth: that God in all things may be glorified through Jesus Christ, to whom be praise and dominion for ever and ever. Amen.

1 PETER 4:11

"MANY PEOPLE KNOW HOW TO CRITICIZE, BUT FEW KNOW HOW TO PRAISE."   **Ethel Waters,**
Singer, Dancer, and Actress

*Trials
and
Troubles*

Promises from God for

Brokenness

It is at these times of helplessness and bro-kenness, when we are in the deepest valleys of hurt and despair, that God's salvation is closest to us, surrounding our heart. Our challenge is to risk opening our broken heart to the healing power of God's love. Our divine partnership is with God in Jesus Christ from everlasting to everlast-ing....God does not want us to be brokenhearted. Wisdom teaches that when a covenant is broken, God offers forgiveness that can heal the wound and love that can mend the broken heart.

K. SMALLWOOD 406-15

"I REFUSED TO BE DISCOURAGED, FOR NEITHER GOD NOR MAN COULD USE A DISCOURAGED SOUL."

Mary McLeod Bethune, Educator

Excerpt from the *Women of Color Study Bible*

The Lord is nigh unto them that are of a broken heart; and saveth such as be of a contrite spirit.

PSALM 34:18

~

Purge me with hyssop, and I shall be clean: wash me, and I shall be whiter than snow. Make me to hear joy and gladness; that the bones which thou hast broken may rejoice. Hide thy face from my sins, and blot out all mine iniquities. Create in me a clean heart, O God; and renew a right spirit within me. Cast me not away from thy presence; and take not thy holy spirit from me.

PSALM 51:7-11

~

It is better to trust in the Lord than to put confidence in man.

PSALM 118:8

~

A merry heart maketh a cheerful countenance: but by sorrow of the heart the spirit is broken.

PROVERBS 15:13

~

As soon as Jesus heard the word that was spoken, he saith unto the ruler of the synagogue, Be not afraid, only believe.

MARK 5:36

Promises from God for

Death

God gives us the courage to trust Him even in the face of death—courage to believe that He is too wise to make a mistake and too good to do wrong. May God continually remind us that this world is not our home. We're only to pitch a tent, not build a homestead (see 2 Corinthians 5:1). And when it's our time, we too will hear a song and cross over.

L. MELTON-DOLBERRY 822-27

Excerpt from the *Women of Color Study Bible*

*For we know that if our earthly house of this
tabernacle were dissolved, we have a building
of God, an house not made with hands,
eternal in the heavens.*

2 CORINTHIANS 5:1

~

*In my Father's house are many mansions: if it
were not so, I would have told you. I go to
prepare a place for you.*

JOHN 14:2

~

*For our conversation is in heaven; from whence
also we look for the Saviour, the Lord
Jesus Christ.*

PHILIPPIANS 3:20

~

*They shall hunger no more, neither thirst any
more; neither shall the sun light on them, nor any
heat. For the Lamb which is in the midst of the
throne shall feed them, and shall lead them unto
living fountains of waters: and God shall wipe
away all tears from their eyes.*

REVELATION 7:16-17

~

*And God shall wipe away all tears from their eyes;
and there shall be no more death, neither sorrow,
nor crying, neither shall there be any more pain:
for the former things are passed away.*

REVELATION 21:4

Promises from God for

Despair

ob's torment is finally ended when he realizes that while God does not promise a rose
garden, God does promise to never forsake
him. What saves Job is that, even in the midst of
his anguish, he continually seeks God for answers.
Job often feels tired and angry with God (Job 9:35),
but he never gives up (Job 10:1-2). He constantly
seeks to maintain his relationship with God (Job 2;
42:2). It is when we are at our lowest that God
hears our cries (Jeremiah 31:15; Matthew 2:18)....
If God is willing to sacrifice His only begotten Son
to save us, surely He will come to our aid in the
midst of our despair. We have only to call on Him.

S. MOLOCK 694-19

Excerpt from the *Women of Color Study Bible*

The Lord is on my side; I will not fear: what
can man do unto me?

PSALM 118:6

❧

Fear thou not; for I am with thee: be not dismayed; for I am thy God: I will strengthen thee;
yea, I will help thee; yea, I will uphold thee with
the right hand of my righteousness.

ISAIAH 41:10

❧

And he said unto me, My grace is sufficient for
thee: for my strength is made perfect in weakness.
Most gladly therefore will I rather glory in
my infirmities, that the power of Christ
may rest upon me.

2 CORINTHIANS 12:9

❧

For God is not unrighteous to forget your work
and labour of love, which ye have shewed
toward his name, in that ye have ministered to
the saints, and do minister.

HEBREWS 6:10

"THE BEST WAY TO FIGHT POVERTY IS WITH A
WEAPON LOADED WITH AMBITION." **Septima Clark,**
Educator

Promises from God for

Discouragement

O ften we utter ardent requests and become discouraged when God's timing does not coincide with our own, and His ways do not surrender to our meager understanding. At these moments, we should "let go" and "let God." It is always better to wait than to force things. God's yoke is easy and God's burden is light (see Matthew 11:28-30). When God directs a situation, we don't have to force circumstances. They flow. Prayer is not intended to be a means of manipulating God, but as a way of seeking God's strength, direction, and will.

C. Archibald 822-32

Excerpt from the *Women of Color Study Bible*

Why art thou cast down, O my soul? and why art thou disquieted within me? hope in God: for I shall yet praise him, who is the health of my countenance, and my God.

PSALM 43:5

~

And he said, Abba, Father, all things are possible unto thee; take away this cup from me: nevertheless not what I will, but what thou wilt.

MARK 14:36

~

Be careful for nothing; but in every thing by prayer and supplication with thanksgiving let your requests be made known unto God. And the peace of God, which passeth all understanding, shall keep your hearts and minds through Christ Jesus.

PHILIPPIANS 4:6-7

~

Rejoice evermore. Pray without ceasing. In every thing give thanks: for this is the will of God in Christ Jesus concerning you.

1 THESSALONIANS 5:16-18

"POSITIVE ANYTHING IS BETTER THAN NEGATIVE NOTHING." **Lorraine Hansberry, Playwright and Activist**

Promises from God for

Fear

Whatever our current circumstances may be, we must refuse to, as theologian Howard Thurman writes, "Allow the events of our life to make us a prisoner." Instead, we must remember that "our lives offer so much more than our immediate experience discloses to us." Harriet Tubman's work was done in the shadows of darkness and evil, but she ultimately prevailed. The apostle Paul urged the passengers on the doomed ship, sailing toward Rome, to "be of good cheer . . . for there stood by me this night the angel of God, whose I am, and whom I serve, saying, Fear not Paul . . . I believe God" (Acts 27:25). So should we.

M. DYSON 406-14

Excerpt from the *Women of Color Study Bible*

I sought the Lord, and he heard me, and delivered me from all my fears. They looked unto him, and were lightened: and their faces were not ashamed.

PSALM 34:4-5

It is God that girdeth me with strength, and maketh my way perfect.

PSALM 18:32

Be of good courage, and he shall strengthen your heart, all ye that hope in the Lord.

PSALM 31:24

For the Lord God will help me; therefore shall I not be confounded: therefore have I set my face like a flint, and I know that I shall not be ashamed.

ISAIAH 50:7

"FEAR IS NOT A WALL BUT AN EMOTION. AND LIKE ALL EMOTIONS, IT CAN BE OVERCOME."

Gwen Goldsby Grant, Psychologist

Promises from God for

Grief

As you begin to recognize the stages of grief, you will learn how to walk and grow through this experience....Grief can only be conquered when it is faced honestly, with divine help and the support of other people. Thank God for the widely available sources of help from family members, friends, ministers, and physicians. After many days of hopelessness, you will learn to live with the memory of your loss. This experience will help you mature and make you better equipped to reach out to others. You can go through this experience with God, who provides all the comfort you'll need.

C. LOVE 822-26

*He restoreth my soul: he leadeth me in the paths
of righteousness for his name's sake. Yea, though I
walk through the valley of the shadow of death, I
will fear no evil: for thou art with me; thy rod
and thy staff they comfort me.*

PSALM 23:3-4

*Evening, and morning, and at noon, will I pray,
and cry aloud: and he shall hear my voice.*

PSALM 55:17

*Hear my cry, O God; attend unto my prayer.
From the end of the earth will I cry unto thee,
when my heart is overwhelmed: lead me to the
rock that is higher than I.*

PSALM 61:1-2

*For if we believe that Jesus died and rose again,
even so them also which sleep in Jesus will
God bring with him.*

1 THESSALONIANS 4:14

"CHARACTER IS WHAT YOU HAVE LEFT WHEN YOU'VE
LOST EVERYTHING ELSE." **Patricia Harris,
Former Secretary, Housing and Urban Development**

Promises from God for

Loneliness

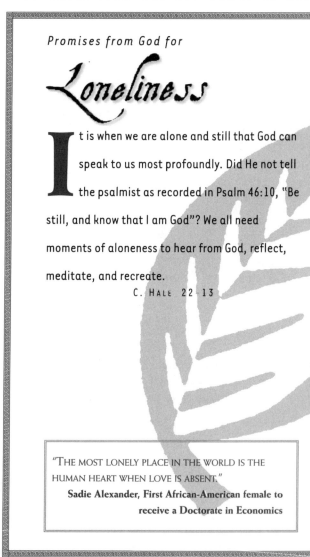

I t is when we are alone and still that God can speak to us most profoundly. Did He not tell the psalmist as recorded in Psalm 46:10, "Be still, and know that I am God"? We all need moments of aloneness to hear from God, reflect, meditate, and recreate.

C. HALE 22 13

"THE MOST LONELY PLACE IN THE WORLD IS THE HUMAN HEART WHEN LOVE IS ABSENT."

Sadie Alexander, First African-American female to receive a Doctorate in Economics

Be still, and know that I am God: I will be exalted among the heathen, I will be exalted in the earth.

PSALM 46:10

❧

The Lord is nigh unto all them that call upon him, to all that call upon him in truth.

PSALM 145:18

❧

That they should seek the Lord, if haply they might feel after him, and find him, though he be not far from every one of us.

ACTS 17:27

❧

Let your conversation be without covetousness; and be content with such things as ye have: for he hath said, I will never leave thee, nor forsake thee.

HEBREWS 13:5

❧

And in the morning, rising up a great while before day, he went out, and departed into a solitary place, and there prayed.

MARK 1:35

Promises from God for

Sorrow

s we seek the Lord with all our heart, we must believe that God is thinking about us and cares for us. We need to feel free to come to God with our pain and sorrow, just as David and Bathsheba did (2 Samuel 12:16). We must believe God has a plan to give us hope and a bright future, and that God will be with us always even in the midst of our deepest pain and sorrow (Jeremiah 29:11:14; Matthew 28:20).

J. THOMPSON 246-15

Excerpt from the *Women of Color Study Bible*

The Lord is nigh unto them that are of a broken heart; and saveth such as be of a contrite spirit.

PSALM 34:18

~

Then shall the virgin rejoice in the dance, both young men and old together: for I will turn their mourning into joy, and will comfort them, and make them rejoice from their sorrow.

JEREMIAH 31:13

~

Blessed be God, even the Father of our Lord Jesus Christ, the Father of mercies, and the God of all comfort; Who comforteth us in all our tribulation, that we may be able to comfort them which are in any trouble, by the comfort wherewith we ourselves are comforted of God.

2 CORINTHIANS 1:3-4

~

Seeing then that we have a great high priest, that is passed into the heavens, Jesus the Son of God, let us hold fast our profession. For we have not an high priest which cannot be touched with the feeling of our infirmities; but was in all points tempted like as we are, yet without sin. Let us therefore come boldly unto the throne of grace, that we may obtain mercy, and find grace to help in time of need.

HEBREWS 4:14-16

Promises from God for

Stress

ecause we are human, distresses will enter into our lives. But if we allow the Lord into our lives, we will have immediate access to the One who not only cares that we are troubled, but is also powerful enough to bring us out of our troubles. Sometimes we make the mistake of believing that when God brings us out of a situation, it will be resolved to our own satisfaction. We assume that God will agree with the way that we think the dilemma should be settled. Often God does not change the circumstances in order to relieve our problems. A change is made in us—in the way we view or react to what is going on around us and inside of us.

A. ADAMS-MORRIS 406-22

Excerpt from the *Women of Color Study Bible*

*Then they cried unto the Lord in their trouble,
and he delivered them out of their distresses.
And he led them forth by the right way, that they
might go to a city of habitation. Oh that men
would praise the Lord for his goodness, and for
his wonderful works to the children of men!
For he satisfieth the longing soul, and filleth
the hungry soul with goodness.*

PSALM 107:6-9

~

*He sent from above, he took me, he drew
me out of many waters.*

PSALM 18:16

~

*Thou hast turned for me my mourning into danc-
ing: thou hast put off my sackcloth, and girded me
with gladness; To the end that my glory may sing
praise to thee, and not be silent. O Lord my God,
I will give thanks unto thee for ever.*

PSALM 30:11-12

~

*In every thing give thanks: for this is the will of
God in Christ Jesus concerning you.*

1 THESSALONIANS 5:18

Promises from God for

Temptation

Everyone will struggle with some kind of temptation throughout the course of her life....However, the example of Jesus Christ and the Word of God teach us how we can overcome temptation. The Bible teaches us that God does not tempt us, but states rather that temptation arises from two sources: our own passions (James 1:13-15), and Satan, often called the "tempter" (Luke 4:2). God allows us to be tempted to teach us obedience, trust, and loyalty to Him. Although being a Christian does not exempt us from experiencing temptation, God does promise not to tempt us beyond what we can bear. Instead He provides a way of escape (1 Corinthians 10:13). Jesus shows us that using the Word of God is an effective means of overcoming temptation (Matthew 4:1-11).

J. THOMPSON   854-31

*Watch and pray, that ye enter not into temptation:
the spirit indeed is willing, but the flesh is weak.*

MATTHEW 26:41

❧

*For the grace of God that bringeth
salvation hath appeared to all men,
Teaching us that, denying ungodliness and
worldly lusts, we should live soberly, righteously,
and godly, in this present world.*

TITUS 2:11-12

❧

*Let no man say when he is tempted, I am tempted
of God: for God cannot be tempted with evil,
neither tempteth he any man:
But every man is tempted, when he is drawn
away of his own lust, and enticed.
Then when lust hath conceived, it bringeth forth
sin: and sin, when it is finished,
bringeth forth death.*

JAMES 1:13-15

❧

*Submit yourselves therefore to God. Resist the
devil, and he will flee from you.*

JAMES 4:7

Promises from God for

Worry

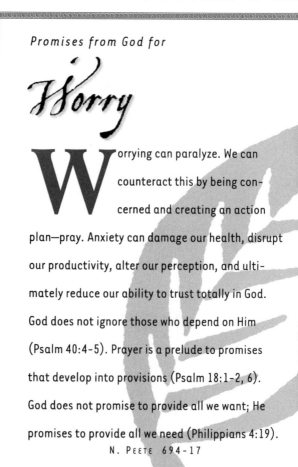

Worrying can paralyze. We can counteract this by being concerned and creating an action plan—pray. Anxiety can damage our health, disrupt our productivity, alter our perception, and ultimately reduce our ability to trust totally in God. God does not ignore those who depend on Him (Psalm 40:4-5). Prayer is a prelude to promises that develop into provisions (Psalm 18:1-2, 6). God does not promise to provide all we want; He promises to provide all we need (Philippians 4:19).

N. PEETE 694-17

> "WORRY IS INTEREST PAID ON TROUBLE BEFORE IT IS DUE." **Miriam Makeba, Folksinger**

And he said, I will love thee, O Lord, my strength.
The Lord is my rock, and my fortress, and my
deliverer; my God, my strength, in whom I will
trust; my buckler, and the horn of my salvation,
and my high tower.

PSALM 18:1-2

Thou art my hiding place; thou shalt preserve me
from trouble; thou shalt compass me about
with songs of deliverance.

PSALM 32:7

Cast thy burden upon the Lord, and he shall sustain
thee: he shall never suffer the righteous to be moved.

PSALM 55:22

But my God shall supply all your need according
to his riches in glory by Christ Jesus.

PHILIPPIANS 4:19

Therefore I say unto you, Take no thought for
your life, what ye shall eat, or what ye shall drink;
nor yet for your body, what ye shall put on. Is not
the life more than meat, and the body than rai-
ment? Behold the fowls of the air: for they sow
not, neither do they reap, nor gather into barns;
yet your heavenly Father feedeth them. Are ye
not much better than they? Which of you by tak-
ing thought can add one cubit unto his stature?

MATTHEW 6:25-28